The Harpers & Queen Guide
to London's 100 Best Restaurants

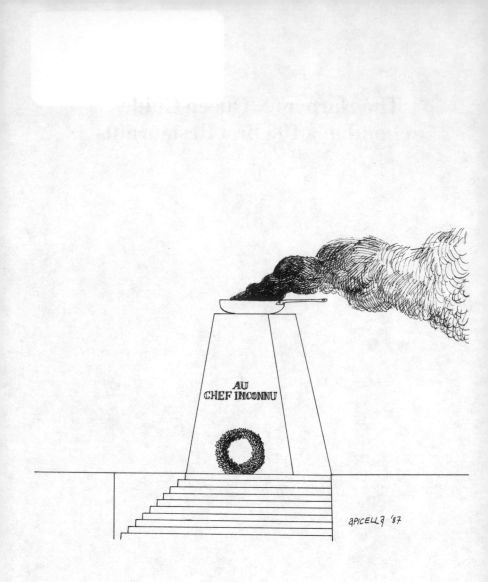

AU
CHEF INCONNU

APICELLA '87

The Harpers & Queen Guide to London's 100 Best Restaurants

LOYD GROSSMAN

Illustrated by Enzo Apicella

Roger Houghton
London

First published 1987
Text © Loyd Grossman 1987
Illustrations on pages ii, 24, 62, 95, 106, 113, 173, 178, © Enzo Apicella 1987;
all other illustrations © *Harpers & Queen* 1987
Cover designed by Craig Dodd

Set in Linotron Dominante by Gee Graphics
Printed and bound in Great Britain by Biddles Ltd, Guildford, Surrey
for Roger Houghton Ltd, in association with J. M. Dent and Sons Ltd,
Aldine House, 33 Welbeck Street, London W1M 8LX

British Library Cataloguing in Publication Data

Grossman, Loyd
    The Harpers & Queen guide to London's 100
    best restaurants.
    1. Restaurants, lunch rooms, etc.—
    England—London—Guide-books   2. London
    (England)—Description—1987-   —
    Guide-books
    I. Title
    647'.95421   TX910.G7

    ISBN 1 85203 018 6

Acknowledgements

The eighteenth-century churchman James Woodforde established the standards of no-nonsense eating out criticism. I particularly like his diary entry for 17 February 1763: 'I dined at the chaplain's table with Pickering and Waring, upon a roasted tongue and udder ... N.B. I shall not dine on a roasted Tongue and Udder again very soon.'

My distinguished predecessors at *Harpers & Queen* have been equally forthright and I am particularly grateful to both Humphrey Lyttleton and Quentin Crewe for the high standards which they established. I am grateful also to Stephen Quinn, publisher of *Harpers & Queen*, for his support and encouragement, to Willie Landels, the founding editor, and to Nicholas Coleridge the current editor. Thanks also to Enzo Apicella for his splendid drawings. My column owes a great deal to the patient and sedulous work of the *Harpers & Queen* sub-editors, over the years notably Patrick O'Connor, Anthony Gardner and Markie Robson-Scott: their own writing and criticism has been most helpful. Thanks to Brooke Auchincloss too.

Finally my thanks go to those who've dined: Jamie Fergusson, John Service, Pandora Wodehouse, Sebastian Whitestone, Laura Kirwan-Taylor, Alan Crompton-Batt, Anita Rothschild, Tim Mercer, Liz Walker, David Profumo, Nicky Beech, Simon Taylor, Sarah Spankie, Willie Lewis, William Joll, Johnny Stirling, Prue Murdoch, Peter Osborne, Jeffery Tolman, Kevin Sim, Nicholas Hely-Hutchinson and most especially Debs.

The indigestion was their own; the judgements and the blame solely mine.

Introduction

This guide is purely subjective. All the restaurants in it have been judged on the basis of personal visits. All restaurants have off days and in some cases I may have visited an establishment when the chef or staff were feeling blue or bolshie. In such cases they have my sympathy, but I'm afraid it's hard cheese for them. Any restaurant that is open to do business is open to be judged. I've never seen a restaurant mark down its prices because the chef felt that he wasn't on top form that day.

All the pieces in this book have been written specially for it, but the method and approach used here has been developed and practised in my restaurant columns in *Harpers & Queens* for five years. Most people recognise that food is only part of the pleasure of eating out – even the most sublime sauce maltaise doesn't make up for appalling service, filthy house wine or uncomfortable chairs. Restaurants, after all, are social theatres as well as watering holes.

The choice of 100 restaurants might sound restrictive – in fact, it's generous. Some of the restaurants in this 'top 100' are, in fact, utterly disgusting, but they are sadly unavoidable. In spite of all the back slapping and self-congratulatory hoo-ha that the food establishment indulges in, a shocking number of London's 'best' restaurants put on a very poor show indeed. Things are getting better, but there's a long way to go.

Much of the general rise in standards is due to the proliferation of 'ethnic' (i.e. not British, French or Italian) restaurants. Indeed these restaurants have done a lot towards keeping eating out cheapish and interesting. Indian and Chinese restaurants have become part of the fabric of everyday dining, but hotter and weirder newcomers, like the current wave of new Thai restaurants, are now where the real ethnic excitement is. Sadly, the quality of cooking in the ethnics tends to be crazily inconsistent, so few of them can be recommended without reservation.

It is pleasing, too, to see a rise in the quality of neighbourhood restaurants. Continental cities have always been distinguished by the number and excellence of their local restaurants, and fortunately, good and well-intentioned restaurateurs are setting up shop all over town. Still, the top restaurants remain overwhelmingly concentrated in a diagonal band that stretches the short distance from Leicester Square to Putney Bridge.

Even though new restaurants seem to be opening in every vacant shopfront – many fuelled by cash from the Business Expansion Scheme – the London restaurant scene is surprisingly static. A restaurant like Langan's or Le Caprice may only open once in every five years; out of all the new restaurants that open each year there may be only the smallest handful of genuinely interesting ones.

Because of the popularity of ethnic and informal restaurants, conventional ratings which either dole out percentage points or stars based on some highly codified system of judgement are really quite irrelevant. So there are no symbols or accolades in this guide. I really would hesitate to declare any restaurant 'the best' in London, but if pushed I would say that I tremendously admire the following: Le Caprice for consistent good humour and glamour, Alistair Little and Hilaire for stylish innovation, Simply Nico for technique, Sweetings for fish, La Pappardelle for pizza, Veeraswamy's for Indian, Langan's for high-class peasant food, The Wine Gallery for being cheap and interesting and the Launceston Place Restaurant for Sunday lunch.

But this is a particularly exciting time to write about restaurants as Londoners are finally abandoning their shyness and conservatism about eating out. Restaurants are an indispensable part of civilised town life and we punters will ultimately get as much or as little as we demand from them.

A note on prices

Prices change so rapidly – always upwards, of course – that giving exact prices is useless. We have indicated relative prices, which include an appropriate wine and service, as follows:

£   Cheapish – £15 a head or less
££   Average – £15 to £25
£££   Expensive – £25 and upwards

It is worth noting that many of the most expensive restaurants offer extremely good value set lunches.

Alistair Little

49 Frith Street,
London W1
Tel: 01-734 5183
Mon-Fri 12.30 to 2.30, 7.30 to 11ish
VISA
££

Good for: *Fish, blowing out gastronomic cobwebs*
Caveats: *Severe chairs*

Voluble, film starry, well educated and just temperamental enough, Alistair Little has unsurprisingly been thrust into the forefront of the great chef-as-pop-idol trend. But the press hype ('Alistair's in the papers more often than Princess Di' one restaurateur grumbled) oughtn't to detract from the fact that Little, along with Simon Hopkinson at Hilaire (*q.v.*), is at the very least the best young chef in London. The tiny dining room – protected from the harsh realities of Soho street life by hi-tech Venetian blinds – is, I suppose, functional modernism. The tables and chairs are black, simple and rather stern. A mass of metal light fixtures, suggestive of the early *Star Trek* school of interior design, populates the Chinese red ceiling. The table settings – a little dish of sea salt, a pepper grinder, plain cutlery and paper napkins – clearly mean business.

With astonishing energy and invention, the menu changes at every lunch and dinner. The style of cooking, sometimes tagged 'new British' or 'modern British', is, I think, a marriage of extreme skill and common sense: the best seasonal ingredients cooked with verve and sensitivity. Soups, which may be cabbage and celeriac or bacon and flageolet, or the stunning seafood consommé with sliced fish are a favoured first course among the brave

1

eclecticism of pappardelle, sashimi and gravadlax. A dish of lightly grilled baby squid stuffed with basil and breadcrumbs was unquestionably one of the best ways to begin a lunch in London. I have always had immense admiration for Little's way with fish: salmon charred on the skin side and just barely cooked on the other side was the most delicious salmon I've ever eaten. Sea bass, which might be steamed with aromatic vegetables, is worth the inevitably high price. *Mirabile dictu* the chicken here – sometimes served with wild mushrooms – actually tastes of something. Liver and beef are always first rate too. There are huge and good seasonal salads. Vegetables are well cooked, trendy (like baby jerusalem artichokes) but served in an irritating communal selection. Puddings are out of this world: rich, seductive and megacalorific like the dark and white chocolate truffle cake or fig and mascarpone tart. The wine list is good and not too punishing. A small troop of girls who appear to be art students provide friendly if somewhat amateurish service. The whole feel of this place is welcomely free from the pretension, fuss and priggishness of so much of London's supposedly 'top class' cookery. You will usually eat memorably here. Lunchtime tends to attract the Sohoesque media gang; dinner is rather more relaxed. The tables for two are overly intimate.

L'Arlequin

123 Queenstown Road,
London SW8
Tel: 01-622 0555
Mon-Fri 12.30 to 2, 7.30 to 10.30
ACCESS, DINERS, VISA
££

Good for: *Set lunches, demanding diners*
Caveats: *Bad for the Bunteresque, excessive gravitas*

Christian Delteil is a young chef with a good pedigree: Le Gavroche and Chewton Glen. He boldly trod in Battersea, and set up his small and pricey restaurant on the doorstep of Chez Nico. After a good start – hard to get into, talked about at drinks parties – he faltered. His restaurant was too sepulchral, his cooking too finicky, his wine prices too too outrageous. The restaurant has now doubled in size, with new decor and, I am pleased to say, a rather more cheerful attitude – most of the worst pedantries of nouvellism have been sent down the Tweeny. Which is not to say that it's become like the Hard Rock Café; no sir, the resurrected L'Arlequin isn't quite a bundle of laughs. It is a serious restaurant in more than one way. There is dragged pistachio woodwork, comfortable *Directoire* chairs and shaded wall sconces. The cutlery is solid, the linen is crisp and the glasses are big. The white-jacketed staff are extremely correct.

Delteil's cooking is correct too and his attention to detail and quality is admirable. There is a first course ragout of artichokes – splendid artichoke bottoms lightly flecked with tomato – which is simple and excellent. The marinated raw salmon is buttery and favourful and garnished with the inevitable seasonal salad. The bread rolls are warm, crisp and chewy as they ought to be. The fish cooking here is outstanding and the unfishy can be top class too. Basic things like roast lamb with thyme are cooked and presented with finesse. A fricassee of pigeon with shallots certainly ranks up there with the best pigeon ever. Vegetables incline perhaps too far towards the 'turned potato and hushed reverence' school of cookery. You are given irritatingly minute, artfully composed little selections of things like sculpted carrots, braised endive and pommes dauphinoise. All quite excellent, but more please. Puddings are top of the form: try the compendious assiette gourmande which sometimes includes an almost killingly rich chocolate marquise.

Fellow diners ranging from local box wallahs to earnest gourmets *font le voyage* to Queenstown Road. Set lunches are relatively cheap and very, very good. A little more levity might not hurt: even the clowns on the menu – 'Expatriate Comedians' by Claude Harrison – look as if they've just received a threatening letter from the bank manager.

Aunties

126 Cleveland Street,
London W1
Tel: 01-387 1548
Mon-Fri 12 to 3, 6 to 11
Sat 6 to 11
ACCESS, AMEX, VISA
££

Good for: *Yuppies searching for roots, smoked mackerel*
Caveats: *Hong Kong tenement seating density*

Of all the restaurants purporting to flog 'authentic' English food, this place probably does it with the most success and the least finicky approach. Not that you can get away entirely from the likes of 'trucklements', 'The Colonel's curried egg mayonnaise' or 'Marhayes Manor tipsy fruit trifle'; it's just that they ain't half as twee as they sound. With the honourable exception of a few Turkish restaurants – The Tower Grill in particular – Post Office Towerland isn't the most fertile place for restaurant goers. Aunties (its previous incarnation was as a tea room, hence the grimaceworthy name) set up shop here in 1960, but it wasn't until 1985 that a chef and owner with serious intent took over. The railway carriage of a dining room has been neatly Edwardianised: bright green paintwork, dark stained woodwork, plush banquettes and moss green walls sporting a selection of sepia photographs. Seating is so intimate that the careless could end up with their elbow in a stranger's trucklements.

Stripped of its hi-ho-ninny-ninny prosody the menu is concise and unfussy. You can begin with a good egg mayonnaise, earthy soup, seasonal salad or, when it's available, dreamy, warm smoked trout. Main courses are traditional, uncomplicated and cooked and presented with a style not normally associated with the homely. Your Barnsley chop will be the biggest and best chop south of the Trent, the chicken stew with dumplings is rich and fresh with a herb dumpling of heroic proportions. Bangers and mash, beef and mushroom pie and the like are among the best in London. The less hearty could have nice fish of the day – there is excellent skate, for example, cooked *en papillote.* Vegetables are *au point.* Puddings are huge, rich, packed with kilocalories and Crikey they're good: it would take a hard man to resist the slightly hyperbolic 'best ever bread and butter pudding'. There are obscure English farmhouse cheeses of excellence and, if you must go the whole hog, some English wines on the list. Service is amiable, the atmosphere surprisingly lively, due perhaps to the growing number of admen who now haunt North Fitzrovia. Shaun Thomson, the young chef who trained with Anton Mosimann (*q.v.* the Dorchester), is worth watching.

Bahn Thai

21a Frith Street,
London W1
Tel: 01-437 8504
Mon–Sat 12 to 2.45, 6 to 11.15
Sun 12.30 to 2.30, 6.30 to 10.30
ACCESS, AMEX, VISA
£

> Good for: *Tickling tired palates, vegetarians*
> Caveats: *Slightly dull atmosphere*

Long before Thai cooking became the fashionable cuisine they say it is, Philip Harris was beating the drum for 'King and I' fodder in his basement restaurant in Marloes Road. That establishment still flourishes, but this new place is proselytising in the West End. It used to be Bianchi's, the well-loved and utterly mediocre Italian restaurant and hangout for Soho literati. Bianchi's is now just a case of indigestion remembered, but the blue plaque identifying this building as the site where John Logie Baird first switched on a telly remains. The decor has been well Thaied up. The ground-floor dining room has comfortable claret-coloured banquettes, wood panelling and a ceiling full of upside-down parasols. Upstairs is less cosy and the site of a very cheap lunchtime buffet; I like downstairs better. You might toy with a Thai cocktail like Tropical Itch (hold the talcum powder) whilst you study the encyclopaedic (125 dishes) menu which is helpful and candid: 'All these sauces tend to be hot and pungent and often not to the taste of non Thais.' Just as well, because even though the waitresses are charming and efficient English is not necessarily their strong point.

First courses are delicately cooked, spiced with conviction and neatly presented on cobalt blue crockery. Beek gai yab sai is a splendid dish of boned chicken wings stuffed with a minced meat and chicken filling, steamed and then given a quick fry to produce irresistibly crunchy skin. I'm very fond of kbratong tong, a group of half a dozen tiny batter cups filled with spicy vegetables; it would be the most sublime cocktail party food. Main courses have finesse and flair too. There is first-rate crab and excellent steamed mussels with chilli and lemon sauce. Chicken laab is a furiously hot concoction of minced chicken, lemon and chilli. Vegetables are crispy and exciting and there is a good selection of bean curd dishes for vegetarians. Thai ice cream is probably the most effective way to soothe the savaged tongue. House wine is good and there is an intelligently composed wine list. The food here is fresh and stimulating: no wonder so many chefs come here on their day off.

Bar Escoba

102 Old Brompton Road,
London SW7
Tel: 01-373 2403
Mon–Sun 9am to 11pm
ACCESS, VISA
£

> Good for: *Bar snacks, surrealism*
> Caveats: *Piped music*

Tapas (Spanish bar snacks: often quite elaborate) are one of those frequently forecast culinary fashions – rather like sushi – whose time has never seemed to come. While Spanish food in this country is disgracefully represented, tapas could offer a fresher and more acceptable approach. Bar Escoba is a jolly, brave and on the whole fairly successful essay in the less Inquisitional aspect of Spanish culture. The mediterranean blue walls are painted with psychedelic crustacea and decorated with appliqué scallop shells; there are odd Gaudiesque iron wall sconces; a Technicolor portrait of Juan Carlos and an upside down photograph of Generalissimo Franco. Thus primed, you are unsurprised by the eccentricities of the menu, which ranges from the chatty ('In Spain tapas eaten before meals are a way of life') to the surreal ('Miro looked into the sky and saw omelettes') to the vaguely minatory ('when you begin to end it is a dangerous time').

Gastronomically the menu romps from breakfast to snacks, lunch to dinner. The tapas are the main attraction and good they are too. A collection spiked with plastic cocktail toothpicks arrives on a communal plate. Paella croquettes (little balls of fried presumably leftover paella), mussels with garlic, eggs tartare (like eggs mayonnaise only slightly more chic) and sardines in tomato and basil are excellent. Astonishingly the olives in garlic and chilli are frightfully dull. Main courses are rather more problematical. There are the old let's-have-dinner-six-months-after-Benidorm standbys, like zarzuela and paella. Grilled fish of the day – dished up on a square plate and garnished with lemon and parsley – is fresh and good; pollo escoba (marinated grilled chicken daubed with a lurid red sauce) is not so hot. The chips are so so and the tomato and onion salads perfunctory. Service is cheerful, breezy and full of advice for the uninitiated. Most of the customers are on the right side of thirty.

La Bastide

50 Greek Street,
London W1
Tel: 01-734 3300
Mon-Fri 12.30 to 2.30, 6 to 11.30
Sat 6 to 11.30
ACCESS, AMEX, DINERS, VISA
££

Good for: *Trenchermen, Armagnac*
Caveats: *Slightly too sedate*

This splendid eighteenth-century house is evocative of the days before Soho became the tit and bum capital of the Empire. Even though you can still buy naughty knickers a short stroll from the front doorstep of any of the new Soho beaneries, the recent burst of restaurantisation – of which La Bastide is a part – is supposed to foreshadow a day when the half square mile will be safe and wholesome for grannies and young families.

Inside this restaurant one certainly feels blameless: the decor and the rather placid atmosphere are all reminiscent of fading hotels in the boondocks of provincial France. The heavy velour drapes, the plushtex upholstered chairs, the dinky chandeliers and the boarded-up fireplace, all hint at a style of cooking that will perhaps owe more to tradition and less to interior decoration than is currently fashionable. Indeed Nick Blacklock, the ex-psychologist in the kitchen, tends to produce dishes which are best described as earthy: good, strong flavours, huge helpings, unfussily put onto plates and sent out to the dining room.

Sometimes a less rough and ready sous chef can produce some strange combinations: excellent salade roscovite – like a smart Russian salad made with prawns, cauliflower and artichokes – was garnished provincial-restaurant style with horrid little cubes of red pepper and placed on a preposterously overblown bed of French leaves. The little cubes of pepper incongruously topped a rich and gutsy crab gratin as well.

Every month or so there is a changing regional menu which is often full of goodies. Brittany produced most excellent gigot: thick slices of perfectly pink good quality lamb and a mountain of white beans in a garlicky tomato sauce. Roast duck with peas looked dull but tasted fresh and honest. Vegetables and salads could use a bit more attention. There is a fairly elaborate à la carte and something called the Soho menu which is, I suppose, rather more cheap and simple. You can eat ogen melon and a fillet steak whilst your companion tucks into andouillettes or foie gras. Puddings are excellent. The wine list is fun and challenging with an enormous selection of French regional wines: the strong of constitution will follow on to the cerebellum-numbing collection of Armagnac. Service from French boys in black ties is friendly if occasionally slightly spaced out. Clientele come mostly from the less flashy end of the Soho population – you will see more suits than sunglasses here.

Beccofino

100 Draycott Avenue,
London SW3
Tel: 01-584 3600
Mon–Sat 12.30 to 2.30, 7 to 11.30
ACCESS, AMEX, VISA
££

> Good for: *Noisy lunches, family dinners, pasta*
> Caveats: *Not much elbow room*

This is probably the best and most useful of the little knot of Italian restaurants clustered around the newly trendy shopping district of 'Brompton Cross'. In a previous life as a French restaurant it was Au Fin Bec (literally 'a fine nose', meaning someone with discerning taste) but the Italian Beccofino refers to the magnificent honker of owner Dante Betti. You pass through a minute bar into a long box of a room whose muddy scrumbled walls are hung with a jumble of paintings ranging from the crudely amateurish to the quite good: there is an excellent copy (I assume) of Manet's portrait of Berthe Morisot. A large central reservation of banal Italian restaurant puddings of the oranges-in-syrup school rouses fears of mediocrity that are thankfully unrealised. The rust-coloured banquettes are comfortable.

The menu is more interesting than most; if you avoid the chicken sorpresa you can eat well-cooked, modestly progressive Italian food made with good ingredients. Easily assembled dishes like ham and melon or tonno e fagioli will at least show a reasonable amount of care: bagna cauda (a good selection of raw vegetables with a hot garlicky dip) is excellent and the huge grilled mushrooms are ideal for the slimmer. More ferocious appetites will like the pasta, which is thoughtfully handled. Penne with chilli and tomato sauce is properly snappy; paglia e fieno with basil and tomato rather gentler. Grilled monkfish is the best bet amongst the half dozen fishy dishes. There is predictable veal with lemon and terrifying chicken breast with asparagus: the veal with tuna sauce, the grilled chicken with herbs and the carpaccio with parmesan are all robust, worthwhile dishes. Vegetables served from those institutional metal ovals are merely okay: a radicchio salad is an altogether better bet. The tightly packed crowd of unseasonably tanned women, chaps who drive fast cars and wandering media moguls bray forcefully enough to discourage eavesdropping – dinner is more sedate. There is a good list of Italian wines with treats like Tignancello San Casciano. Service is brisk and inevitably jocular: 'Is that your Rolls Royce parked outside today?' Espresso is good; graffiti in the loos unrepeatable except perhaps for the modestly scrawled 'Down with Comprehensive Schools'.

Blakes Hotel Restaurant

33 Roland Gardens,
London SW7
Tel: 01-370 6701
Mon-Sun 12.30 to 2.30, 7.30 to 11.30
ACCESS, AMEX, DINERS, VISA
£££

Good for: *Seduction, power-broking, visiting Americans' expense accounts* Caveats: *Over-priced wine, snotty reception*

Blakes is one of the very few special restaurants in London – grown-up, glamorous and exciting, rather like its owner

Oz dolly bird turned entrepreneur Anouska Hempel, wife of financial whiz Mark Weinberg. The Hempeled basement bar and dining room is ferociously chic and unritzy. Before dinner you can get sozzled in the splendour of an oriental-screen-lined alcove or in the fashionable gloom of the chrome-and-black bar where Dire Straits seeps from the Tannoys. Cannily lit Himalayan tribal costumes in perspex boxes punctuate the stark mostly black (including the fire extinguisher) decor. The table settings are superb: masses of fresh flowers, splendid wine glasses, rock salt and Szechuan peppercorns in swirly glass bowls, excellent cutlery. Fellow guests are unsurprisingly rich and international moguls of post-industrial businesses like pop, film, design and telly. Louche in the nicest possible way, it is an arch seduction joint for the established, though an incredulous friend actually saw a man dining with his own wife here. Patrice, the stellar Tunisian manager, has gone and one's greeting can be an unappetising mixture of unction and duplicity. 'I'm just going to put you at a special table,' the manager said agreeably before installing me in a corner virtually under the stairs. Service by a fleet of stylish girls who look like extras in a James Bond movie is charming and efficient.

You can munch excellent guacamole and tortilla chips whilst studying the loonily eclectic menu with its Russian-Italian-Chinese-Japanese-English-French influences. Try not to notice the heart-stopping prices. No wonder the woman in shades at the next table looks nervous: what is *he* going to want in return for a £10.75 foie gras salad? Cooking is on top form, though perhaps not as good as it used to be. The chicken tikka is succulent and gutsy: ravioli with hazelnuts in a fresh tomato and coriander sauce is unorthodox, but first rate. The fish, like salmon in pastry with ginger, is always good news as are the noisettes of venison with celeriac. The Szechuan duck with roasted salt and pepper is not quite as wonderful as it ought to be. The pommes dauphinoise are exemplary; the vegetables fresh

13

and just crunchy enough; the wild rice wildly expensive and unadulterated. Helpings are huge and desserts – even the excellent sorbets or the Grand Marnier soufflé – unachievable. Coffee is, of course, served with smart goodies like fondant cape gooseberries. The wine list is genuinely overpriced: house white is an unstaggermaking £9.50 a bottle. But even though the bill is hefty you do get what you pay for: good ingredients, adventurously cooked in an atmosphere of rather privileged sophistication.

The Bombay Brasserie

Courtfield Close,
Courtfield Road,
London SW7
Tel: 01-370 4040
Mon-Sun 12.30 to 2.30, 7.30 to 12
ACCESS, AMEX, DINERS, VISA
££

> Good for: *Mid-winter blues, romantic dinners,*
> *cheap lunchtime buffet*
> Caveats: *Spaced-out waiters*

To quote the handsome and hefty menu: 'Bombay. The Gateway to India. Then. As now ... The Bombay Brasserie attempts to capture the spirit of Bombay with a menu that reflects its cosmopolitan character and is culled from the very finest of India's exciting and varied cuisines. Here you will find the sumptuous cuisine of the Moghul Emperors, wholesome Punjabi fare, the earthy delights of the Tandoor or clay ovens, the fish dishes of Goa's golden coast, the robust cuisine of the northwest frontier . . . and more, in an environment with the ambience of an age gone by.' Well, aside from the purple prose there's very little wrong with this place. Sometimes the waiters appear to be contemplating the transient nature of earthly existence and sometimes unfamiliar customers will be treated with polite disdain, but for most people, most of the 365 days a year this restaurant is open, the Bombay Brasserie is unquestionably the best, grandest and most expensive Indian restaurant in London. It has been conceived on an epic scale and in spite of opening in the wake of *Gandhi* and the *Jewel in the Crown* it purveys the atmosphere of a comfortable and benevolent Raj in which the ceiling fans whirr smoothly and the glasses are never empty.

There is a huge and comfortable bar where you may wait longer than expected before reaching your table. The main dining room is splendidly high ceilinged with big cane chairs, brass and wood service stations and a Kewsworth of potted palms. The raw silk papered walls are hung with sepia photographs of Victorian Bombay bourgeoisie. Table settings are correct with stiff dusty rose nappery and the biggest wine glasses ever; the plates are huge too.

As in every other Indian restaurant in the world you can begin with chicken tikka, which will be better than any you've ever had. The adventurous could choose boned quail stuffed with lamb pilaf, a potentially tricky little number cooked and served with verve and sensitivity. Tandoori dishes are exceptional, especially the lamb chops with ginger which are a triumph of polyethnicity – 'French-cut English lamb cooked Indian style.' Some of the Parsi dishes are more surprising, like sali botti – a bowl of rich mutton and apricot stew wearing a hat of straw potatoes. Masala prawns are giant, succulent and hot. Chicken xakuti could blow the tongue out of a blue whale, they aren't timid with their spicing. The various thalis (a selection of little dishes presented on a large round metal tray) are ideal for the greedy; vegetarians are well looked after by the spicy Punjabi thali. All the vegetable dishes are cooked to an extremely high standard, as are the breads

15

and the fried brown rice. Puddings are, alas, *de trop* but the sorbets, particularly the chocolate, are the best in London. The walking wounded may risk a lethal and complex concoction called Cobra coffee as an after-dinner treat. A pianist proficiently ripples through the likes of 'These Foolish Things' and 'Your Mother Should Know'. There's also a large conservatory dining room with tile floor, trompe-l'oeil murals and candlelight: rather better for serious pre-snog curries. House white is so so – Kingfisher beer is advised.

British Harvest

London Hilton,
Park Lane,
London W1
Tel: 01-493 8000
Mon–Sun 12 to 2.45, 6 to 10.30
£££

> Good for: *Aunt Ethel from Omaha*
> Caveats: *Lacks spirit*

Why are there so few jokes about food? Because chefs don't tell jokes; they cook them. Or so it seems at the much vaunted British Harvest restaurant, an establishment frequently cited as proof of the new pride in British cookery. You enter a windowless room carved from the bowels of the Hilton, harsh and cheerless like the lobby of a faded station hotel. A menu illustrated with Stubbs' *Harvesters* and choked with hideous verbiage is presented. You want smoked salmon? Why not have 'home smoked farm salmon fished from the sea lochs of Scotland' instead. Or how about a sandwich? 'It is commonly believed that the sandwich was invented by the Earl of Sandwich on 6th August 1762'. On menus like this 'gratuities' are of course always 'at the discretion of the guest'. It all adds up to a coy and 'refeened' gastronomic romp from Land's End to John o' Groats.

You may well wish to begin with 'Omelette Wellington – our speciality omelette'. Fair enough, Apsley House is a stone's throw away and maybe the Iron Duke was partial to the odd egg. What exactly is omelette Wellington, you ask the waiter. 'Kidney omelette,' he replies. 'Is it good?' you ask. 'If you like kidneys,' he replies losing patience. You'd have to like kidneys an awful lot to swallow the mess which arrives: blindingly yellow eggs harshly cooked and filled with stewed kidneys in a thick brown sauce. When you order rack of lamb the waiter may, like mine, ask if you want it medium or well done as they used to ask twenty years ago. When the rack of lamb arrives it may be in a horrid cream of rosemary sauce. Steamed breast of chicken with – you guessed it – 'garden fresh vegetables' is a better bet. An accompanying selection of – wait for it – 'garden fresh vegetables' was a fairly mediocre plate of chicory, mangetout and mushrooms. At a neighbouring table a quartet of dull besuited foreigners were tucking into much more appetising-looking roast beef. The beef, you will be pleased to know, comes with – I can't bear the suspense – 'garden fresh vegetables'. There is an enterprising assortment of British cheeses and coffee is served with excellent shortbread and brandy snaps. Drink from the commendable choice of British wines; the French wines on the list are stratospherically priced. Service is sullen and inept.

The Five Iron Laws of Eating Out

1 Avoid restaurants where the waitresses dress like Nell Gwyn

2 Never go to a restaurant which advertises home cooking

3 The quality of a restaurant is inversely proportional to the number of steps you have to climb to get to it

4 The more frequently your waiter interrupts with 'Who's having the fish?' the less likely it is that that person will get the fish

5 If the maitre d' jokes about not having frogs' legs or chicken wings because after all he's only human, get up and go.

Bubb's

329 Central Market,
London EC1
Tel: 01-236 2435
Mon-Fri 12.15 to 2.30, 7 to 9.30
NO CREDIT CARDS
££

> Good for: *After walking tours of Smithfields, beleaguered journalists*
> Caveats: *Sloppy cooking*

They say that before long, Smithfields will be Covent-gardenised and H.R. Jones's awesome market halls will soon house shops selling cashmere pullovers and sweaters with sheep on them. I hope not. But before the evil day arrives, enjoy what remains of the meat market: the tranquillity of St Bartholomew the Great (surely the most beautiful parish church in London) and the aloof grandeur of Thomas Gibbs' gateway to St Bart's hospital. There is plenty of refreshment in the area: the not-quite-up-to-scratch fish at Rutland and Stubbs, the huge breakfasts and gargantuan steaks at the Fox and Anchor and the French fodder at Bubb's. It is hardly a *restaurant du quartier* – there are few signs of market culture here – but there are lots of journalists and 'marketing' men. Sometimes there is an almighty kerfuffle of misplaced reservations and misspelled names at the bar-cum-reception desk. Waiters will interrogate you, smile and vanish. Somehow you eventually reach your table. If you're a twosome you will be able to taste your neighbour's cigar, smell his aftershave and hear about the break-up of his marriage. Fours have rather more spacious seating.

The menu is short and not particularly interesting but supplemented by a reasonable number of daily specials.

You might begin with a smooth and unobjectionable chicken liver pâté foolishly set in a puddle of what looks like cocktail sauce and turns out to be some absurd glop of red pepper. A gratin of mussels and whitefish is rich, savoury and enough for two. Soups are good. Main courses are sloppy and haphazard, ranging on a limited scale from okay to not bad. An irreproachably cooked piece of the freshest possible haddock is smothered in mediocre hollandaise and left blistering under the heat lamps. A huge entrecôte is *au point* and tasty until doused with greasy and poorly made marchand du vin sauce: they obviously buy far better than they sauce here. Vegetables are disgraceful. Puddings and cheese are all right, as is the coffee. House wine could be improved. In spite of the gastronomic horrors it's not such a bad place and one fears that they trade disgracefully on the location and ambience to get away with such thuggish cooking. The textured wallpaper, the *sang de boeuf* paintwork and the Gauguin poster are all the stuff of Gallic dreams; why not try harder in the kitchen?

Café Bouchon

362 Kings Road,
London SW3
Tel: 01-352 0074
Mon-Sat 12 to 2.30, 7 to 12.30
Sun 12 to 2.30, 7 to 11.30
ACCESS, AMEX, DINERS, VISA
££

> Good for: *Midnight feasts, real Maine lobsters*
> Caveats: *Tough on slimmers*

More than a hundred years ago, in the depths of the Haute Savoie, Monsieur Bouchon invented a sauce of legendary savour. He passed the secret recipe to each of his six daughters and sent them to establish far-flung steak houses. Or so they say. At any rate a distant relation of Monsieur Bouchon armed with the esoteric formula has set up shop in the Kings Road. The little dining room is cosy and functional with a quarry tile floor, paper tablecloths, rudimentary cutlery and little red-shaded table lamps. Photographs of nineteenth-century Bouchons dot the walls.

The menu is commendably straightforward. One of their excellent salads probably makes the best first course: there is watercress and orange with first-rate vinaigrette or a green salad garnished with almonds and sliced hard-boiled egg. The centrepiece of lunch or dinner is the entrecôte Bouchon, a vast and exceptionally good hunk of beef carved into thin slices and presented on an oval platter with a more than liberal serving of bubbling sauce Bouchon. The sauce – close to a Café de Paris sauce – is garlicky and good. If not perhaps for the purist who likes his meat charred and unadorned, I think it may be the best steak in town. There are huge helpings of pommes alumettes or jacket potatoes with sour cream. They've recently begun serving fresh Maine lobsters flown in from America. They present them cold, split in half and garnished with salad, lemon and mayonnaise: they are wonderfully sweet and tasty. In their honour a red plastic lobster now dangles in the front window. Puddings are simple – apple or straw-berry tart or Brobdingnagian coupes of sorbet. Coffee from *cafetières* is the real thing. The wine list could stand a bit of improvement. Service by a minute team is courteous and efficient. Sometimes the piano music – *Cabaret, Gigi* and the like – can be a bit irritating.

The Camden Brasserie

216 Camden High Street,
London NW1
Tel: 01–482 2114
Mon–Sat 12 to 3, 6.30 to 11.30
Sun 12 to 3, 6 to 10.30
NO CREDIT CARDS
£

> Good for: *Massive grills, before Camden Lock*
> Caveats: *Emotional TV-am producers complaining about ratings/management/unions*

If owning a television station is a licence to print money, owning a restaurant close to a television station is close to a licence to print money. The panjandrums of the telly world (like their colleagues in advertising or publishing) work so hard that they even work at lunchtime. And there's so much work to do that their working lunches must be long and arduous ones. Whilst you could always score some credible falafel in street cred Camden Town it wasn't until

TV-am set up shop in 1983 that restaurants began to flourish there. Old-established neighbourhood watering holes like the once moribund Devonshire Arms were given a new lease of life and smartish restaurants like this one mushroomed in the shadow of the Terry Farrel designed TV-am headquarters. They have come (Le Bistroquet) and gone (Pancho and Lefties) but this place has remained a bustling focal point of Camden Town eating. Its success is completely unsurprising – after all who wouldn't take advantage of a restaurant that was this jolly, cheap, accommodating and good? Decor is bistro standard – brick walls, oilskin tablecloths, framed photographs of the dubious charms of Camden Town street life. On cold days a fire blazes. There is a small bar where you can perch whilst waiting for a table.

The menu is straightforward; the cooking fresh and simple. There is good homely soup to start with or coppa salami with proper olive oil or maybe the usually okay pasta of the day. The spicy chicken wings are too finicky – more action than satisfaction really. The salade niçoise is huge and excellent. Main courses are all straight off the charcoal grill. Steak brochette teriyaki is disappointing, the fish of the day is fresh and cooked to a turn. Beef is perhaps best, the rib of beef satisfies even the most ferocious. Everything is served up with good pommes frites and the side salads use good produce, well dressed. The cheese board is good enough to demand another bottle from the fairly priced wine list. Service from waiters and waitresses, who look as if they're playing waiters and waitresses in a telly play, is hip and gets the job done. A sister restaurant downstairs, the Pasta Underground, serves up cheap and stylish pasta in post-modernist surroundings.

APICELLA '87

La Capannina

24 Romilly Street,
London W1
Tel: 01-437 2473
Mon–Fri 12 to 3, 6 to 11.30
Sat 6 to 11.30
ACCESS, AMEX, DINERS, VISA
££

> Good for: *Arriving admen, Soho atmosphere, before*
> *Ronnie Scott's*
> Caveats: *Italian clichés*

Is there any other restaurant in London where you could hear someone actually saying: 'It is very good for the soul when young to sell advertising space'? La Capannina is probably the prime lunchtime bolthole for the Filofax and Frascati set, so if you're an aspiring copywriter, focus puller or video director the cheek-to-jowl tables here might provide you with some useful contacts. The sheer unstylishness of the place – compared that is with the other Soho hotspots the admen like – has turned it into an advertising industry canteen whose antediluvian decor (q.v. L'Epicure just across the road) endows the 'little cabin' with a sort of street cred. It somehow feels like the 'real' Soho of the Colin MacInnes era. So you won't be surprised by the rough plaster walls and the cacciatori impedimenta (a profusion of flintlocks) or the copper pans or the fiasci of Chianti. There is of course a groaning hors-d'oeuvre trolley replete with overdressed crab, egg mayonnaise, stuffed mushrooms and whitebait.

The menu is predictable and rather quaint – if you like, you can have stracciatella and chicken sorpresa. The prose is quaint too: 'spaghetti mantecated with eggs, bacon and cheese'. Sorry, but you did say 'mantecated' didn't you? Alas, the word doesn't figure in my *Chambers* and the dish must remain a mystery. The straightforward cookery is perfectly adequate, the frills inept. You will be given a large and slightly overboiled artichoke which will then be mugged by appalling vinaigrette. The crespolini and cannelloni will be volcanically hot and comfortingly gungy if bearing little relation to fine Italian cooking. More offbeat dishes like the rabbit stew or the pigeon are handled with assurance; the old familiar ones have a regrettably unloved quality. Fish is not as good as it ought to be. Vegetables, overcooked and over-buttered, deserve more respect. The jolly and efficient staff are perhaps too imbued with the old-fashioned willingness to brandish a pepper grinder at any opportunity. 'If you're not careful,' a friend said, 'they'll pepper the tablecloth as you sit down.' But it is hectic and fun even if a few too many customers do have a habit of calling for 'il conto'.

Capital Hotel Restaurant

Basil Street,
London SW3
Tel: 01-589 5171
Mon-Sat 7 to 10, 12.30 to 2.15, 6.30 to 10.15
Sun 7 to 10.15, 12.30 to 2, 7 to 10
ACCESS, AMEX, DINERS, VISA
£££

> Good for: *Visiting classical impresarios, greedy godparents*
> Caveats: *Ultra dull surroundings, overwrought food*

Along with Blakes, the Capital Hotel restaurant was one of
the first new hotel dining rooms to attract acclaim and
custom, quite an achievement considering that apart from
the indisputable attractions of eating at the Savoy, the
Dorchester, the Connaught or Claridge's, Londoners don't
much fancy hotel dining rooms. While Blakes went for
jet-set naughtiness and hiply progressive cookery, the
Capital opted for a staid but outstanding approach combining dull decor, correct service and highly impressive
cooking from then-chef Brian Turner. Accolades followed.
Well, Turner is now gone and the dining room is redecorated. The bland modern box of a room overlooking Basil
Street has been fairly effectively dressed in *avant le deluge*
style with Louis Quinze chairs covered in floral needle-
point and great flower-stuffed vases trompe-l'oeiled on the
walls. The clientele is rich and well upholstered to match
the decor.

The menu is pretentious and absurd: 'Si par hasard un
plat manquait à cette carte c'est uniquement parce que
nous ne disposerions pas d'elements assez rigoureusement
frais pour le préparer aujourd'hui.' In other words everything is fresh, and so it should be when you are paying

£14.00 for a grilled sole. The cooking here is extremely refined and capable though slightly predictable and I fear ultimately rather pointless. Many of the shibboleths of post-nouvelle cookery can be found here, like lukewarm salad (salade de pêcheurs tiède au Xeres' – relax though, it's a salad of fish rather than fishermen) or old standbys turned on their gastronomic heads (so steak tartare becomes 'tartare de deux saumons'): and jolly good they are too, though this sort of cooking tends to fall at the second hurdle. So, oddly enough, 'quenelles de poisson fumé' – rather sophisticated smoked fish dumplings – didn't taste all that different from a delicately cooked chicken breast stuffed with roquefort mousse. It all tastes and looks rather nice with its sweet little garnishes and artfully smooth puddlets of beurre blanc, but there seems to be an overwhelming feeling of well-mannered blandness. Vegetables are well treated. Potatoes get rather full blown baroquery: little croquettes with a crispy golden skin modelled to look like miniature apples. The piggy will enjoy white chocolate marquise with coffee sauce. The wine list is long and most bottles dwell in the £20 plus atmosphere, although there is a small list of cheaper wines ('quelques vins qui ne sont pas sans mérite' as we say in Knightsbridge) appended to the menu. Thankfully Badoit is poured *ad libitum*.

Le Caprice

Arlington House,
Arlington Street,
London SW1
Tel: 01-629 2239
Mon-Fri 12 to 2.30, 6 to 12
Sat 7 to 12
Sun 12 to 3, 7 to 12
ACCESS, AMEX, DINERS, VISA
££

Good for: *Late nights, long lunches*
Caveats: *Noisy*

This place has more genuine celebrities per square foot than any restaurant in town but if some people knock it for its fashionability, the food has never taken a back seat here, although the kitchen does sometimes bend under pressure. The decor by Eva Jiricna was once revolutionary but has now settled into unobtrusive chicness. The black tiles, furniture and woodwork, the white walls and Venetian blinds have aged well as have David Bailey's moody photographs of the famous – Malcolm Muggeridge, Catherine Deneuve, Mick Jagger – which glower down on diners. The long and crowded bar, always bracketed by sensationally abstract flower arrangements, displays a compendium of the world's hootch and produces the best Bloody Mary in London.

The short menu is a miracle of accommodation: everyone can always find something on it. Fashion harpies may spend a long lunch toying with the crudités while trenchermen tuck into grilled veal sausages and sautéed potatoes. Charles Fontaine, who I think is a much underrated chef, toys with eclecticism and usually pulls it off. So you can have credible bang bang chicken or tagliolini with mushrooms. Blissful raw salmon marinated in lime juice, scrambled eggs (topped with salmon roe) and smoked salmon and the eggs benedict are all stellar first courses alongside the by-now-trademark huge bowl of crudités. Fresh tuna salad – when it's on – is frightfully good, the Caesar salad, alas, frightful. Main courses run the gamut of complexity. The hamburger (chopped steak to the nobs who write this menu) is splendid and served up with a bowl of London's outstanding pommes allumettes. The grilled duck breast in various guises and the grilled calves' liver with shallot sauce are exemplars of good, fresh no-nonsense cookery. Fish is generally well handled (either grilled, steamed or sometimes in an excellent fish cassoulet) although the titanic salmon fishcake is rather disappointing. Lobster, when it makes an appearance, is top class. Vegetables are crisply cooked. The most irresistible pudding is the white and dark chocolate mousse. House wine is good and cheap, smartish bottles generally stay below the £20 mark and there are nine interesting rosés on offer. Espresso and cappuccino are excellent and they provide four sorts of tea. Service is swift and friendly, the front-of-house team, headed by owners Chris Corbin and Jeremy King, vigilant and welcoming: cooking good; presentation unfussy; bills controllable; no wonder it's so hard to get into. New Yorkophiles will love the Sunday brunch, an oasis of noise in the peace of a West End Sunday.

Le Casino

77 Lower Sloane Street,
London SW1
Tel: 01-730 3313
Mon-Sun 24 hours
VISA
£

> Good for: *Pre-dawn hunger pains, cheapskates*
> Caveats: *Food*

Peter Ilic has been much praised for his inventiveness and low prices. He is a mine of often loony sounding approaches to food (his menu for the future) and restaurateurship (his restaurant where the customer pays what he thinks his food and drink is worth), but he has flourished and now controls five London restaurants. While some punters rave about his rock bottom prices I can't help thinking that his restaurants – at least the two that I've been to – are based on a formula which reduces to the fact that people will stand for almost anything, provided that it's cheap enough. I unquestionably ate the worst dinner of my London life at the Pigeon, his Fulham establishment.

Le Casino occupies the former site of a gaming club that did a brisk trade in attracting young hooray degenerates. The idea behind it is a good one – a cheap and cheerful twenty-four-hour-a-day joint serving slap-up breakfasts, lunches, tea, dinner and after-party munchies. It is hard keeping a twenty-four-hour-a-day joint clean. It might look okay after a few litres of liebfraumilch at Amanda's flat when one's popped round here to soak up the booze, but in the cruel and sober light of day, oh boy. The decor is beatnik-folk-club round straw table mats, wine bottles encased in candle wax, knotty pine wainscoting. The carpet is the dirtiest I have ever seen in a place where food is served. Fairly spaced out hip chicks dispense what I suppose could be charitably called 'casual' service. In a fairly empty restaurant I waited just over fifty minutes (that's right 50) for a smoked chicken salad. Ample time I suppose to study my fellow lunchers, a sophisticated lot ... ('Brian's just got a job working at Lewisham town hall.' 'Is that so?' 'Really, Lewisham.' 'Really.') By the time the salad arrived one had totally lost interest, but it was, I suppose, okay. A tomato omelette was a fairly revolting, barely whisked mess of overcooked egg and a few bits of tomato. An unctuous white-patent-leather-shoe-clad manager eyed our scarcely eaten food with that sort of 'concern' that makes you want to hide in a corner and gag. The house wine is cheap.

The Champagne Exchange

17c Curzon Street,
London W1
Tel: 01-493 4490
Mon-Fri 11.30 to 3, 5.30 to 12
Sat 5.30 to 12
Sun 7 to 11
ACCESS, AMEX, DINERS, VISA
£

> Good for: *Late-afternoon trysting, blinis*
> Caveats: *Bland surroundings*

There are remarkably few decent places to eat in Mayfair, particularly if you're not long on hours and overdrafts. Shepherd Market is now supporting a worthy gaggle of increasingly good Turkish and Middle Eastern restaurants which do the trick, but if you want some easy and uncrippling glamour this is the place. Its slick international VIP lounge modernism is a bit of a shock amongst the stately doorways of Curzon Street. Through the glass and chrome entrance you're in to a cool grey world where sophisticated jazz is in the air and champagne (lots of it) on ice. The place is designed to within an inch of its life and I find the decor – grey walls, overly bright spotlights, lacquered chairs, designer lithographs – the most misguided thing about the whole restaurant. Still . . . the linen is pukka and the cutlery is hefty. The menu and place plates are marbleised.

Although there are a few sometimes ambitious dishes of the day, this place is really more of a bar than a restaurant and all the food is perfect champagne-soaking fodder. So there's a good array of smoked fish – salmon, halibut, sturgeon – and a decent selection of caviar. You can have your fishy snacks on their own or with blini – Russian buckwheat pancakes served with melted butter and soured cream – or baked potatoes or scrambled eggs. Helpings and prices are pretty reasonable. If you want to build the semblance of a conventional lunch or dinner you could begin with fish soup or decent vegetable soup and finish with chocolate truffle cake or hot fruit crumble. Champagne comes by the glass, three different sizes ranging from the coy Tsarina to the numbing half pint, or in a wide selection of bottles; they even have three sorts of still champagne. Prices range from the decent house by Jacques Martin at £14.50 a bottle to the plutocratic '78 Dom Pérignon Rosé at £110. Your neighbours will be sleekly suited entrepreneurs and fierce blondes weighed down with Louis Vuitton. Waiters in black waistcoats and long white aprons wait efficiently.

The Chanterelle

119 Old Brompton Road,
London SW7
Tel: 01-373 5522
Mon-Sun 12 to 2.30, 7 to 11.30
ACCESS, AMEX, DINERS, VISA
£

> Good for: *Cheap lunches, aging trendies*
> Caveats: *Perfunctory service*

Without being patronising, I think, this restaurant, designed by the youthful Terence Conran, is most remarkable as a survival of the sixties. The long and narrow room has both a breezy atmosphere and memories of the brave restauration days when the culinary precepts of Elizabeth David were first being presented to the parents of today's yuppies. The food and the decor have worn surprisingly well. It is a pleasant enough place to be with its rattan chairs, pines, panelling, broccoli green paintwork, leaded glass and Edwardianesque mirrors – just like the one Amanda has above the fireplace in Clapham. There is, of course, a ceiling fan and a large Welsh dresser chockablock with biscuit jars, coffee pots and assorted crockery. Nappery is white paper, cutlery is basic, plates are white (not octagonal) and unadorned.

The food is just as functional and vaguely Frenchified. Indeed this kitchen turns out good, unfussy and not particularly imaginative food of the sort that makes for a sometimes welcome relief. Soups are good: fresh asparagus, for example, is properly creamy without being cloying and with enough stray bits of plant to let you know that this is indeed the real thing. Or you might begin with something like a flavourful and unsophisticated crab mousse. Main courses are slightly reminiscent of the bourgeois dinner party too. There is excellent braised oxtail with red grapes (not at all outlandish) and for a trifling £1.00 surcharge on the set menu you will get a most excellent entrecôte steak. Sometimes they serve cassoulet and there is blanquette de veau and good fish too. Vegetables are served family style and in abundance. Puddings, like the apple and raisin

crumble, incline towards the English school of sweet and satisfying. The wine list is concise and priced with what sometimes seems like nostalgic fairness. The set lunch at £7.00 for three courses is astonishingly cheap in what is now a very high-rent district. Waiters in white shirts and long aprons serve with a combination of hauteur and world weariness.

Le Chef

41 Connaught Street,
London W2
Tel: 01–402 7761
Tues–Fri 12.30 to 2.30, 7 to 11.30
Sat 7 to 11
ACCESS, AMEX, VISA
££

> Good for: *Escapism, dating*
> Caveats: *Poor house wine*

This place has long ploughed its modest furrow of basic French cookery served up in an atmosphere suggestive of La Belle France's less flashy establishments. It was once, no doubt, more exciting than it is now, but it still has plenty of charm and decent fodder to offer. In its bull's-blood-painted shopfront this place presents a slightly down-at-heel appearance – inside it's nicely shabby. There are bare board floors, anaglyptesque chipboard walls, peeling chocolate brown paintwork, flowers in superannuated mustard pots and painted kitchen chairs for seating. The walls are hung with maps of 'les Vignobles de France', cheap tourist prints of Paris, Gallic injunctions about the desirability of wine drinking and the lack of responsibility for customers' coats. The upstairs dining room bustles, downstairs is perhaps *un peu plus* sexy.

The menu is short and hints more at solidity than excitement: you won't be shocked by the nouvellesque here. You might kick off with some escargots or a decent terrine or a tomato salad. The moules are fat and served up in a nicely creamy sauce. The canonical first course must be the famous fish soup. A huge serving bowl of it arrives and you ladle as much as you like; fiercely garlicky rouille, croûtons, and grated cheese come on the side. It's a splendid winter warmer if not always up to benchmark standard. There's a handful of respectable main courses. The entrecôte is huge, nicely cooked, topped with herby butter and dished up with crunchy straw potatoes. Veal and lamb are good too, but it's not particularly a place for the fishy. Vegetables are okay. The cheeseboard is excellent; the house red really ought to be better. Service is charming, informal and generous. The clientele ranges from old regulars to young locals and enjoyment is usually in the air. The piped jazz is as neatly dated as the cooking.

Chez Gerard

31 Dover Street,
London W1
Tel: 01-499 8171
Mon-Sat 12 to 2.45, 7 to 11
ACCESS, AMEX, VISA
££

> Good for: *Friendly lunches, chateaubriand*
> Caveats: *Staff froideur*

The French philosopher Lévi-Strauss wrote that eating a steak imbues man with a bull-like strength. Whilst Anglo Saxons don't easily swallow such Gallic claptrap they don't make such good steak and chips either. There are two sorts of French steak joints trading in London these days: the first is new fangled (like the Café Bouchon, *q.v.*, or Rowleys) and serves sliced steak with a garlicky sauce; the second, like Chez Gerard, is more elemental and dishes up beef the way it comes from the butcher. These are not places for vegetarians or the delicate of constitution. The Chez Gerard formula – a few first courses then grilled steak or lamb and huge bowls of chips – has worked well: there are now three Chezs. Charlotte Street, the original and best, suffered an inexplicable decline when it moved across the road to larger premises; Chancery Lane has frankly never been any good but Dover Street is rambling, bustling and usually does the trick. You enter the dining room past a huge old-fashioned charcoal grill manned by crazed French grill chefs shoving steaks off and on and communicating with a lack of politesse. Indeed most of the staff at all three Chezs, though efficient, appear to be suffering from some form of charisma bypass.

First courses tend to be composed rather than cooked and are generous and use decent raw materials: you might begin with a platter of smoked halibut/mackerel/sprat/ tuna with horseradish sauce or a salad niçoise or a simpler salad of tomatoes and basil. Steaks are bought from a good supplier and treated with respect. Your steak will arrive exactly as ordered and it will be large and flavourful. Likewise your lamb cutlets will be nicely pink and smack neither of the freezer nor of Chernobyl. The pommes frites are not the best in London, but they are jolly good anyway. There are no vegetables. Fish may turn up as a daily special and it will be serviceable enough. The wine list is perhaps rather too concise: those gargantuan steaks could occasionally justify some rather more interesting drinking. There are adequate cheeses and chocolate mousses for the greedy. Coffee is strong and good. In the summer there is a tiny roof terrace; in the winter the banquettes near the front door afford the warmth of the grill and a close look at the affluent pedestrians of Dover Street. The sauce Béarnaise, by the way, is ghastly.

Clarke's

124 Kensington Church Street,
London W8
Tel: 01-221 9225
Mon–Sat 12.30 to 2, 7.30 to 10
ACCESS, VISA
££

> Good for: *Superlative lunches, loony cheeses*
> Caveats: *A bit high-handed*

At night you are given what Sally Clarke has decided to serve: all right at a private dinner party, but not I think what you go out for – and pay through the nose for to boot. I find the authoritarian restaurateur lark – 'I've been to the market and they had lovely brains so brains are what you get' – *passé* and slightly objectionable. Dull, too: you go out to bicker over the menu and look at what your friend and neighbours are eating. But this rather serious quibble aside, it's hard not to be impressed by this restaurant, which in its finer moments offers some of the best and most interesting cooking in town. Go, if you can at lunchtime though, that's when Sally Clarke cooks *and* offers you a choice. A lunch here is a good excuse as well for a window shop in the Ken Church Street antiqueries. At dinner Sally hosts and, I feel, dictates.

The unpromising store front premises have been well done up with bare board floors, ceiling fan and Hockney prints. First courses might be stellar salads – like flageolets verts, french beans, anchovies and fennel – or a selection of delicious new-American-cookery style grilled vegetables. Breads liberally offered are fantastically good. Sally Clarke excels at the innovative, unfussy use of top whack ingredients: dull-sounding dishes tend to be a revelation.

Grilled chicken with shallot butter sauce is flawless as are the accompanying vegetables: sliced summer squash, carrots and broccoli. A could-be-pedestrian lamb chop is expertly butterflied, wondrously well cooked and served up with a zingy redcurrant embellishment. Recherché and perfect English cheeses are served with immaculate home-made biscuits. Puddings – like nectarine tart – are refreshingly uncloying, drawing on English tradition without being swamped by it. Coffee comes in *cafetières* with those irregular lumps of designer sugar. The china is ghastly; the clientele is drawn at lunch from the less commercial end of the publishing world, at night from the more socially glittering cohorts of north of the park London. With Hilaire and Alistair Little (both *q.v.*) this place is the best of the newer generation London restaurants. Less curt service would make it even better.

Coates Café

45 London Wall,
London EC2
Tel: 01–256 5148
Mon–Fri 7am to 8.30 pm
ACCESS, AMEX, DINERS, VISA
£

Good for: *Social City lunching, pop videos, breakfast*
Caveats: *Very noisy*

The surprisingly unstaid firm of Corney & Barrow (est. 1785, wine merchants to H.M., Prince Charles and the Queen Mother) have done more to change the eating habits of City Johnnies than anyone else in the Square Mile. In 1983 they commissioned fashionable architect Julyan Wickam (cele-brated for his work at the Zanzibar – favoured watering hole of trendy media piss artists) to design their flagship restaurant in Moorgate. For this fourth establishment of theirs, they went to Tchaik Chassay, Wickam's collaborator at Zanzibar. C & B's City restaurants have been architec-turally adventurous and gastronomically progressive as well. At a time when most City restaurants were 'pur-veying' game pie and Stilton to the pinstriped segment of the population, C & B were proselytising for rather more modern food and subverting traditional City taste with brash newcomers like beurre blanc and radicchio. Sur-prisingly the restaurants flourished even though the cooking was sometimes shaky and the prices astronomical.

Coates Café is certainly one of the most interesting restaurants to open in London for a long time and perhaps the first recognition that the post Big Bang hi-tech City is anything but fogeyesque. The decor is certainly jazzy: grey metal chairs with springy plastic upholstery, black rubber table mats (very Joseph Pour la Maison) exposed service ducts and splattered paintwork. The bank of large video screens displays a mind-numbing combination of financial information and pop videos. The short menu gingerly treads between the nouvelle and the normal, so you might find 'avocado and orange salad with a dill yoghurt dressing' alongside solid roast beef. The cooking is simple and pretty darned good with the odd excursion into unreality. There is a plate of good mixed smoked fish or a tomato and mozzarella salad in which the mozzarella has been irritatingly diced. The smoked chicken with avocado is foolishly marred by a sweet gloppy orange sauce with the consistency of Dulux. The steaks are excellent and a more adventurous dish like stir-fried pork with green noodles was praised. The wine list is sharp and concise: house champagne is £10.95 a bottle, or you can drink a minor under-age claret for £6.75. If you have to celebrate Sharon-from-the-post-room's birthday, the bar can produce Slow Comfortable Screws, Pink Elephants and Golden Dreams but beware the steep steps to the loos. Service by a team of Australian waitresses is cheerful and chatty-uppy. There is a takeaway shop by the front door so you can pick up dinner as well. They serve breakfast, lunch and evening drinks and it's all fun and cheap too.

The Connaught Grill Room

Carlos Place,
London W1
Tel: 01-499 7070
Mon-Fri 12.30 to 2, 6 to 10.15
ACCESS
£££

> Good for: *Intimate celebrations, hearty eaters*
> Caveats: *Check with bank manager first*

Few things set well-bred hearts racing with excitement more than an invitation to lunch or dinner at the Connaught. It is just that indefinable shade more special than any of its competitors: the London hotel *par excellence*. Even though your fellow diners are likely to be Burberry wrapped and whingeing about oil futures, dual nationality or Concorde, not a shade of vulgarity has intruded into either of the dignified restaurants here. They both share the same kitchen and the same chef, the splendid Michel Bourdin. The Restaurant with its sober wood panelling is bigger and has set price menus, the Grill Room is smaller and perhaps just a tiny bit more pampering. The decor is low key and so well mannered that the dark green and gilt woodwork is scarcely noticeable. There are a few looking-glasses, an indifferent oil of a man on a horse and a scattering of brass wall sconces. Table settings are old grand hotel style: a plate heaped with melba toast (is any other food so evocative?), a pepper grinder, and a three shakers filled with salt, pepper and cayenne. The crockery with its mingy little fake Adamesque design is disgraceful.

The menu is a long and treat-laden document presenting a combination of very grand classical cooking (e.g. noisettes d'agneau Edward VII) and rather rustic English dishes. The list of daily specials (steak, kidney and mushroom pie, boiled silverside, braised gammon) seems to demand a pint of ale instead of a bottle of Lafite. Even the most boring-sounding first courses are apotheosised by the best ingredients and deft cooking, so something like feuilleté of asparagus is heavenly. The 'mosaique' of crab, lobster and langoustines is tangy and refreshing. The 'potages et oeufs' section is thick with dropped names: consommé en gelée Cole Porter, omelette Arnold Bennett, oeuf en gelée Stendhal. There is a heartland of grills and roasts and an excellent array of game in season. Bourdin's cooking is powerful and doesn't beat about the bush. Something like braised oxtail with chestnuts is dark, aromatic and deeply satisfying. Coulibiac is a hefty slice served up with a brace of sauces. Presentation is old fashioned – no sprigs of dill or little mounds of diced tomato here. Vegetables can be a bit clapped out. Puddings arrive on a trolley – anathema to the restaurant progressives. The crème brûlée with raspberries and the bread and butter pudding are utterly wonderful. Tail-coated captains and white-jacketed waiters patrol the tiny room acting with speed, courtesy and friendliness. Prices are dizzying: where else could you pay £3.15 for mashed potatoes?

About Wine . . .

Wine service is one of the most unsatisfactory aspects of eating out. Hearts sink when an unwieldy leatherette-bound carte des vins is presented by an imperious wine waiter. Too many restaurant lists show a singular lack of imagination except when it comes to prices.

Buying expensive wines in all but a very few restaurants is not a good idea (even if you're trying to score points with guests) because of generally inadequate information in wine lists and complete ignorance about how the wine has been stored or handled. A careful search may reveal modestly satisfying wines – some people suggest invariably choosing the second or third least expensive wine on the list, but I don't think this always works.

Otherwise one is thrown back on 'house', which thankfully seems to be getting better and receiving better treatment in more restaurants. A named house wine – i.e. not one that is called 'vin du patron' – is almost always better than an anonymous one. If you're not sure, ask the wine waiter what the house wine is. If he waffles and doesn't give a proper answer, stick to water.

Once you have ordered the wine some restaurants act as if you have only got it on loan. Waiters are either too assiduous or lackadaisical about pouring. I've paid for the stuff: why can't I pour it as I choose?

Daquise

20 Thurloe Street,
London SW7
Tel: 01–589 6117
Mon–Sun 10 am to 11.30 pm
VISA
£

> Good for: *Lone lunchers, the undernourished*
> Caveats: *Bad for slimmers*

This place looks and feels like Eastern Europe: it has long been a prime hangout for the Polish community in exile and foreign students stricken with nostalgie de la café. The ground-floor dining room is bright with fifties decorations – a painting of horseguards in the rain, a coloured paper cut-out of the state coach at the coronation – a patriotic nod of thanks to the host country. This is where the footsore and the regulars come for coffee and cakes or lunch and gossip at the back tables. Downstairs is rather more luxurious: good for dinner or special occasions. The tiny basement dining room seems like a stateroom on a fifties Baltic steamer with neat wood panelling, spruce banquettes and utility chairs. The tablecloths are pink and the crockery institutional. Condiment cum napkin holders are ultra Festival of Britain. There are framed examples of what I can only assume is Polish folk art on the wall.

The menu features homely Polish cookery with an occasional tentative foray – like spaghetti bolognese – into the 'continental' style. Soups are the thing to start with; encyclopaedic Ukrainian borscht (they spell it barszcs) or fabulously good tomato soup. Main courses are earthy: roast chicken, goulash, various sausages. Helpings are huge. You might get two heroic slabs of boiled beef with a creamy sauce or a large neatly sautéed veal escalope topped with a fried egg. My favourite vegetables are the wonderful kasza (steamed buckwheat) and the pickled cucumbers. There are good omelettes and oeufs florentines too. Puddings are mostly from the strudel family. The wine list is rudimentary, the vodka list more exciting. The Tartra beer from the Zywiec brewery ('famous for the production of top quality beer since the fourteenth century') is excellent. Service from waitresses in 'ethnic' dress is harried upstairs, charming below. This is one of the most modest and familial restaurants in town, where lone diners are happily allowed to relax and read, and is an ideal haven after the rigours of pounding the corridors of the V&A.

The Dorchester Terrace Room

Park Lane,
London, W1
Tel: 01-629 8888
Mon–Sat 6 to 11
ACCESS, AMEX, DINERS, VISA
£££

Good for: *Impressing anyone, plutocratic slimmers*
Caveats: *Wrinklies on dance floor*

Sometimes Anton Mosimann's technique is almost blinding in its precision. His deft manipulation of the most precious materials recalls the work of the satellite assembly technician. Mosimann's influence and celebrity is a testament to both great talent and astonishing energy. Almost from the day he arrived at the Dorchester – at the dazzlingly young age of twenty-nine – he has been the most famous chef in the country, beaming at us from box and bookstall. Unlike the Grill where Mosimann turns out robust English food, this dining room is exotic, exquisite and slightly over the top. Decor is oriental tart's boudoir style with a proliferation of elaborate fretwork screens, murals of frolicking mandarins, Technicolor columns and miles of rucherie. Detailing is superb: the little tablelamps have beautiful japanned shades. A slightly incongruous quartet glides through the likes of 'Strangers in the Night' whilst a bevy of black-tied waiters soothingly attend you.

A little amuse-gueule – maybe a slice of warm sausage in brioche dough – arrives while you toy with the large, lengthy and terrifyingly expensive menu. There is a set dinner for the indecisive and a six-course 'menu surprise' based on the day's marketing. First courses are subtle perfection. Slices of warm breast of pheasant are exactly cooked and served with a smartly leafed seasonal salad. There is meltingly tender marinated salmon served with a herb and yoghurt dressing. Fish – like John Dory with braised fennel or steamed sea bass with sliced Chinese mushrooms – is first-class if perhaps a little timidly spiced. The bass, by the way, is an example of Mosimann's recently developed 'cuisine naturelle', to quote the menu 'a cooking technique which uses no cream, no butter, no oil, no alcohol and the minimum amount of sugar and salt'. And it works well, too: poached fillet of beef with a light mustard sauce is wonderfully tender and well flavoured. Vegetables, perhaps baby ears of corn or the tiniest broccoli florets, are cooked with great sensitivity. Puddings are restrained, but seductive. I find some of the menu prose like 'symphonie de sorbets' posey and irritating. Sometimes the clientele inclines too much towards the 'international', but this is one of the country's great dining rooms and when you're feeling rich and indulgent dinner here is the most tremendous treat. Mosimann is a subtle chef with tremendous discipline and a superb staff: he must be the Dorchester's greatest asset.

L'Epicure

28 Frith Street,
London W1
Tel: 01-437 2829
Mon-Fri 12 to 2.30, 6 to 11.15
Sat 6 to 11.15
ACCESS, AMEX, DINERS, VISA
££

> Good for: *Pre-Filofax Soho atmosphere, savouries*
> Caveats: *Not before jogging*

Like its neighbour across the road, La Capannina (*q.v.*), this restaurant's utter disregard for fashion has made it popular with admen and pop music honchos seeking, I suppose, occasional relief from dragged dados and pan-fried brill. The food and service here are as old fashioned as the decor: mid-fifties I should think and rather pleasantly shabby. There is a flaming torchère over the front door which more than hints at the prominent place that the spirit lamp holds in the L'Epicure cookbook. The menu is extremely long and representative of what used to be called 'Continental' cuisine, it is peppered with red dots indicating 'these dishes are cooked on the lamps'. If you want a dish 'cooked on the lamps' you might have saucissons polonais au poivre vert: 'Polish-style sausages sautéed in butter, green peppers, demi-glace and cream served on creamed potatoes' or perhaps Entrecôte Aphrodite: 'Entrecôte steak thinly sliced with mustard flamed with brandy, onion and Worcester Sauce'. It is probably best to wait until after your annual check-up before coming here as these mountains of butter, cream and booze might have the actuaries bumping up your premiums. But it's not all architectonic constructions here. The potted shrimps, or to give them their due, the

Crevettes Alphonso ('potted shrimps tossed in butter with mushrooms . . .' blah blah blah) are exceedingly good as is the gravadlax and the marinated herrings served with warm potato salad and a glass of oesophagus-shocking aquavit. Fish is good if sometimes over garnished, but the skate in black butter and the smoked haddock with a poached egg are just the ticket when you need a bit of gastronomic cuddling. They cook game well in the most straightforward way: the partridge and the grouse are worth having when they pop up on the daily recommendations as are some of the more off-the-wall dishes like stefado (a Greek stew with baby onions) of hare. Puddings are as loaded with cream and alcohol as some of the main courses – the savoury list (mushrooms on toast, chicken livers wrapped in bacon, scrambled eggs with anchovies and Welsh rarebit) is a treat though. There are six sorts of coffee. Service from proper grown-up waiters in jackets is dignified though sometimes a bit creaky around the edges; diners sometimes get demented searching for their long lost aperitifs. The front dining room with its plush banquettes and high density seating is the place to be. The gents' loo is the size of a ballroom and has a good selection of newspapers.

L'Escargot

48 Greek Street,
London W1
Tel: 01-437 2879
Mon-Fri 12.30 to 2.30, 6.30 to 11.15
Sat 6.30 to 11.15
ACCESS, AMEX, DINERS, VISA
££

Good for: *Fish, visiting architects* Caveats: *Not enough plain food*

There has been much talk lately about the revival of Soho, and even though it's still hardly the place to take Granny for a stroll it is steadily turning into an area where entertainment no longer means just a game of hide-the-salami. It seems that as soon as an establishment selling marital aids closes another one opens flogging mosaique de légumes with tomato coulis. For Soho is now yuppie restaurant land *par excellence*. It was really L'Escargot which kicked the whole phenomenon off. Nick Lander turned this grand but moribund Soho institution into a highly fashionable restaurant with the aid of Tom Brent's interior decoration, then chef Alistair Little's cooking and, perhaps most importantly, the social and managerial skills of Elena, who was for many years the celebrated manageress of Bianchi's. It has been a roaring success since the word go, and deservedly so even if there are some avoidable hiccoughs. The decor of pale green ragged walls, the witty carpet woven with snails and snail tracks and vaguely deco furniture has worn well. The ground-floor brasserie (cheapish and hectic) and the two upstairs dining rooms (the top floor has a spectacular barrel-vaulted ceiling, but the first floor, where Elena is, is the place to be) have a pleasant lived-in feel, now that some of the designer edge has worn down.

The menu has been toned down a bit too: there was a stage when it appeared that outlandish marriages and promiscuous stuffing (this is Soho after all) were going to be the rule of the day. Chef Martin Lam has now come up with a menu which is fashionable enough for the pop video makers but avoids most of the boobytraps of post-nouvelle cooking. First courses are fresh and light and good. There might be a well-thought-out and assembled salad of radicchio, oak leaf lettuce, red cabbage and celeriac rémoulade or maybe a well-cooked chicken consommé with quenelles. There is chicken, beef and duck all of which are good enough, but fish is probably the most rewarding main course here. You may get turbot in beurre blanc with little turned vegetables and a sprig of dill: predictable sounding, but sensitively cooked. As will be your sole with ginger and spring onions or the sea bass. Vegetables served on little half moon plates are more thoughtful (for example courgettes with sesame seeds, carrot and parsnip purée) than the average selection. Puddings are first class. The severe will restrict themselves to one of the famous snailshaped chocolates. The wine list (compiled by Jancis Robinson, the owner's wife) is a pleasure to drink and read. One wine is described as 'particularly good value because the labels came off in a collector's cellar'.

L'Etoile

30 Charlotte Street,
London W1
Tel: 01-636 7189
Mon-Fri 12.30 to 2.30, 7 to 10.30
ACCESS, AMEX, DINERS, VISA
££

> Good for: *Civilised ambience*
> Caveats: *Gently declining cooking*

This is one of the last trolley and tuxedo joints – one of those restaurants where everything is displayed, delivered and removed on trolleys by a bewildering hierarchy of staff in different coloured dinner jackets. Fortunately it does enough business to survive without a preservation order. In times past, L'Etoile had rooms as well – the menu still says 'Hotel et restaurant'. Charles Laughton had a bedroom here and the painter Nina Hamnett, 'the Queen of Bohemia', would sometimes nip upstairs for a quick bonk with a new 'discovery'. But the real bohemians frequented the Tour Eiffel across the road. Alas, Augustus John et al weren't assiduous billpayers and the Tour folded. L'Etoile, patronised by rich publishers, carried on. The rich publishers are still here and so are a legion of telly moguls and would-be telly moguls (Channel 4 is just up the road). The dining rooms are splendidly antiquated. There is a pseudo-Turkish fitted carpet, a blood-red dado and creamy textured walls hung with ornamental plates. The rear dining room is divided from the front by a splendid ornamental glass screen etched with representations of the good things in life – like leaping salmon and champagne in ice buckets. The crockery, cutlery and the salt and pepper shakers are all emblazoned 'L'Etoile'.

The menu is heroic and almost archaeological: where else could you find turbot à la monégasque, homard à la russe and escalope de veau à la zingara? The hors d'oeuvre trolley groans under the weight of marinated trout, cold lobster and salade niçoise. The aforementioned turbot à la monégasque is unexciting but okay – a salad of cold turbot served with a dollop of fiercely garlicked mayonnaise. The dressed crab is good, the niçoise heavy handed. Main courses are a mixed bag too. Grilled sole is decently cooked, goujons of the same fish are averagely good, entre-côte chasseur is sloppily sauced and undistinguished. Things like roast grouse are well cooked. Vegetables from a huge selection are overcooked and poorly presented in huge platefuls. The sweet trolley (current *bête noire* of progressive cooking) is a calorific juggernaut of chocolate, cream and displays of fruit. The most modest request is responded to lavishly: 'just a few grapes' produced a wading pool sized bowl of grapes in iced water. Coffee is served from pre-Habitat style *cafetières* and accompanied by a little basket of chocolates. Service is welcoming and deft; the recitation of hors d'oeuvre mind boggling; the sales patter – 'I think you will find that very palatable indeed' – charming.

L'Express

16 Sloane Street,
London SW1
Tel: 01-235 9869
Mon-Sat 9.30 to 5
Sun 11 to 6
ACCESS, AMEX, DINERS, VISA
£

> Good for: *Shopping fatigue, posing, salads*
> Caveats: *Wear comfortable shoes for long queuing*

Darling, schlepping all those bags full of Kenzo and Aza-
dina Alaia hither and yon through Knightsbridge without so
much as a leaf of lamb's lettuce or a glass of Sancerre for
sustenance is so exhausting . . . Unsurprising then that rag
trade king pin Joseph Ettedgui should open a high-class caff
to feed and water SW1 shopaholics. It is, of course, immensely successful – huge queues of the well-shod-and-
dressed crowd the staircase – it is also rather good. Joseph
has a long-standing interest in restaurants, he helped
launch the Caprice, and this place succeeds in giving the
punters the food they want in surroundings well designed
to show off their frocks. Eva Jiricna – the architect who
designed Le Caprice as well as most of Joseph's shops – has
managed to turn this unprepossessing railway carriage of a
basement into a chic, unfussy and ultimately rather exciting place to be. The sleek black woodwork of the mirrored bar with its well-arranged ranks of Perrier and Coca
Cola bottles, the Mallet Stevens chairs (now the *de rigueur*
seating for well-dressed dining rooms) and the air of stylish
minimalism are all nicely deflated by the standard French
café table settings.

The menu is short, frightfully *au courant* and basically
healthful without being preachy: you can expect lots of

APICELLY '87

salads and little alcohol, but thankfully no gastronomic hair shirts. The Virgin Marys and Pina Coladas come in tall Pilsner glasses. The salads are the real things, unlike the tired efforts produced by so many London restaurants. Mozzarella, avocado and tomato means good mozzarella, beefy doorsteps of tomato and a huge clump of basil. The salade niçoise is substantial and full of the goodies you expect: chunks of tuna, anchovies, boiled potatoes, french beans, hard-boiled eggs and designer lettuce. Those who feel they're just too thin will love the granary bread and the piggy puddings. The coffee is excellent: service by white-shirted and black-tied boys and girls can display discomforting alacrity on busy days. The lonely fashionable eat at the bar. Sadly the similar Joseph/Jiricna essay Joe's Café in Draycott Avenue is more belaboured and pretentious: some enlightened tinkering could help. Until then stick to Sloane Street.

About Fads and Fashions . . .

Restaurants aren't held hostage by any rule of good taste: they have their fads and fashions too. Grand old institutions like pudding and hors d'oeuvre trolleys are being slowly swept away as is the tradition of silver service (where the waiter dishes out your food) in favour of plate service where the chef more or less artfully arranges your plate in the kitchen. Indeed, things are swinging more and more in favour of the chef – not always a good thing. The rising popularity of the chef's walkabout – when the man in white roams the dining room interrogating customers – seems, to me at least, a bad and embarrassing practice; I prefer my chefs in the kitchen.

Foods go 'in' and 'out' as well: last year we had vegetable terrine and guinea fowl with raspberry vinegar; this year jerusalem artichoke soup and pan-fried brill with oranges. Will next year bring even more tortured fantasy to our plates? At least nouvelle is cooling in the grave. It seems certain that the ethnic boom will continue and that Southeast Asian places will spring up in every neighbourhood. The so-called new British cooking will probably curb its early excesses and settle down to something more like the modish peasant food that is beginning to find favour around the world. So, after our stomach- and wallet-trying bout with the excessive invention of the last few years, it's going to be back to basics with clear, comprehensible flavours less baroquely decorated food and – praise the Lord – no more high-class baby food.

Fortnum & Mason's St James's Restaurant

181 Piccadilly,
London W1
Tel: 01-734 8040
Mon-Fri 9 to 5
Sat 9 to 4.30
ACCESS, AMEX, DINERS, VISA
£

> Good for: *Godparents up from country, game pie*
> Caveats: *Fred and Stella from Omaha at next-door table*

Unsullied by Philistine changes below – the closing down of the Spanish bar, the almost vandalistic redecoration of the Fountain to something looking like a VIP lounge in a Gulf States airport – this by now creaky ark of gentility sails on. It is one of the very few places which is not a club to have a cheapish, immensely civilised lunch in Piccadilly. The setting is pretty darned grand: ionic columns, rococo-esque wallpaper, Georgianesque columns. The walls are adorned with a fine collection of revivalist (a polite way of saying not as old as they should be) ship pictures. Luridily lit Montague Dawson clippers plough through seas of virginally white foam and famous tea ships race (*Ariel vs. Taieping*) all neatly lit by gallery-style picture lights. My favourite is a wreckage-strewn evocation of the closing hours of Trafalgar: a naked Mademoiselle (her clothes of course having been blown off in the furore of combat in the age of fighting sail) floats on a bit of wreckage in the foreground. Ooh la la.

The menu seems just as teasing and historicist with its section headed 'farinaceous'. Much frequented by young fogeyesque art dealers and more thoughtful American tourists, this is a perfect feeding spot for bluff and proper English food. First courses are mercifully uncomplex: smoked salmon, avocado (filled with prawns of course) or unpotted shrimp. The chicken consommé is excellent but comes without cheese straws: what vile iniquity. Downstairs in tourist class they still get them. A white-suited and high-hatted carver wheels a massive silver trolley round the room dispensing huge helpings of picture perfect beef and all the statutory trimmings. There are equally good alternatives like a homemadish chicken and mushroom pie with rich sauce and buttery crust or cold game pie or that most Fortnumesque concoction Chicken Mexicaine. Fish – grilled sole or fried plaice – is decently done. Vegetables, the crunchy peas excepted, are canteenish. A huge pudding trolley bears fruit tarts, meringues with chestnut cream or chocolate gateau, all exemplars and worthy of a grant from the Sugar Council. The wine list is okay: house carafes do the job. Slowish lunchers get a bonus: the first Burberry clad visitors arrive for tea by three and a grande dame at the piano serenades them with 'As Time Goes By' while you mop up your claret. Never may it change.

Foxtrot Oscar

79 Royal Hospital Road,
London SW3
Tel: 01-352 7179
Mon-Sun 12.30 to 2.30, 7.30 to 11
ACCESS, VISA
£

> Good for: *Lunch after the morning after, girls together*
> Caveats: *Dangerous cocktails*

Few restaurants in London are as well sited for before and after lunch rambles as this one halfway between Wren's Chelsea Hospital and the delightful Chelsea Physic Garden. But such surroundings hardly mean that this joint is full of retired brigadiers and rose fanciers. *Au contraire*, this is a prime playground for the perpetually tanned and the young and noisy. It has somehow always been more than just a neighbourhood hangout and perhaps the length and excellence of the cocktail list – they still make the best bullshot in town – has something to do with it. (Brave drinkers might want to try The Molly Parkin, a malignant-sounding concoction of champagne, triple sec and Southern Comfort.) Decor is a fairly basic pastiche of hipness *passé*: cane chairs, bare brick walls, ferns in baskets.

The menu, displayed on a huge blackboard, ranges deftly from smartish to nursery food so even the most finicky eaters can always find something to pick on between Molly Parkins. Standards of cooking vary: basic is usually best, but sometimes slightly more complicated dishes can be surprisingly good. I like it for easy lunches off the King's Road (more of a restaurant desert than ever). If you want you can start off or even finish with clam fries (not quite the same as fried clams but a reasonable substitute) or loch fyne kippers or tacos. There are decent club sandwiches, stolid shepherd's pie and kedgeree and proficient omelettes. There are good salads and hamburgers too. The wine list is casual and cheapish. Service from apparently teenaged waitresses is a mixture of the friendly and the haphazard. Try to get a table on the ground floor: the basement dining room is dismal.

The Gandhi Cottage

57 Westbourne Grove,
London W2
Tel: 01-221 9396
Mon-Sun 12 to 3, 6 to 12
ACCESS, AMEX, DINERS, VISA
££

> Good for: *Chicken livers, Sunday evenings*
> Caveats: *Too well mannered*

Would the Mahatma find it amusing or irritating to be immortalised in a *bon ton* Westbourne Grove establishment? The tribute is sincere, the menu quoting, 'Non-violence is a rule of conduct for society if it is to live consistently with human dignity and make progress towards the attainment of peace.' The style of this place is definitely post Raj, shunning the Simlaesque fantasies of the Bombay Brasserie and presenting us with a slightly bizarre decorative tribute to someone's idea of English country house taste. The smart little bar has squashy sofas covered in stripy fabric, a neat doric half column is stranded along the wall in the ground-floor dining room, there are enough little crystal chandeliers to furnish half a dozen Mecca ballrooms, and a number of rather cloying pictures of birds disporting in nest and on branch. Chairs are plush and comfortable, the atmosphere slightly hushed and perhaps a little too self-consciously smart. There is an even more glamorous upstairs dining room which doesn't get much use.

The menu is only slightly more adventurous than most but the cooking shows real finesse and some first-rate shopping for produce. Chicken liver masala is mild, flavourful and surprising enough to signal clever goings on in the kitchen. A potentially boring tandoori mixed grill is cooked absolutely *au point*. There is a splendid raw onion and mint chutney. Chicken tikka masala, the standby of Westbourne Grove Indian restaurants, is succulent and buttery. They do an excellent vegetarian thali here: a round tray bearing little metal dishes of spinach bhajee, okra, potato, cauliflower and dal – wonderfully creamy and not lethally garlicked. Indeed if the spicing here errs it is on the side of mildness. The kitchen shows more politesse than ferocity although there's a marked fondness for ginger. The service can occasionally be irritatingly courteous, no waiter seems capable of filling a glass without asking 'More wine, sir?', so don't come here to negotiate custody rights. Indian puddings are up to scratch if you like that sort of thing and there is good home-made ice cream. I am convinced that there is a huge tank beneath central London where coffee stews endlessly before being piped to all Indian restaurants, including this one.

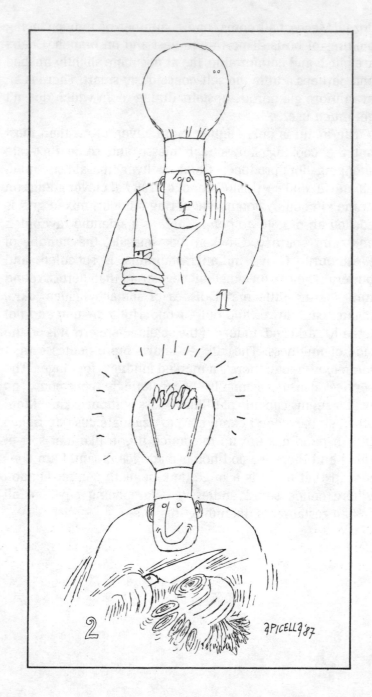

The Gay Hussar

2 Greek Street,
London W1
Tel: 01-437 0973
Mon–Sat 12.30 to 2, 5.30 to 10.30
NO CREDIT CARDS
££

> Good for: *Affluent lefties, hungry people*
> Caveats: *Not before tennis*

Even in post-porn Soho the name is evocative of young men in naughty uniforms, but this establishment purveys the altogether more innocent delights of Hungarian cookery. Although Greek Street has the densest restaurant population of any place in the kingdom, the Gay Hussar stands well above its fellow restaurants – including the other Hungarian one almost next door – in dignity, grandeur and sheer style. Whether the massive helpings of pre-anorexic food is to everyone's taste these days is another matter. The box car of a ground floor dining room is sombrely decorated in mock Tudor panelling enlivened here and there with bits of Hungarian pottery. Seating is mostly side by side on plush banquettes not necessarily designed for the personally over-upholstered. And if your elbow does land in your neighbour's goulash he will probably be one of the old school Labour grandees or political journalists who frequent this place. There is an upstairs dining room but who uses it or why remains a mystery.

Splendidly courteous waiters in dinner jackets present you with the huge menu cheerfully emblazoned with Jol Enni (Eat Well) Jol Inni (Drink Well) Jol Elni (Live Well) and you will do all here, if somewhat heavily. Received standard Hungarian dishes like goulash or chicken papri-

63

kash are on the menu, well executed and only the beginning of the story. There is bright pink cold cherry soup to begin with, or tartly refreshing jellied borscht or the famous fish salad – which is more of a pâté really. The protein starved may want a cold vegetable and sausage salad. Main courses run the gamut from lurid (pink trout with green sauce) to arcane (scrambled eggs with kidneys and brains) and enticing (roast saddle of carp). My favourite is the heroic minced goose (best described as a gooseburger) with slowly stewed beans. Throughout all the cooking here, flavours are fresh and direct and there is a complete lack of gimmickry and pretension. Vegetables are mostly of the cabbage/potato school. Puddings are sweet pancakes or soft fruit salad. The wine list (long on interesting Hungarians and lethally sweet Tokays) is embellished with quotations *à la* 'Dip him in the river who loves water', William Blake. Lunch is amazingly cheap. Any of the staff or best of all the venerable proprietor Victor Sassie will cheerfully advise and explain.

Geales

2 Farmer Street,
London W8
Tel: 01-727 7969
Tues-Fri 12 to 3, 6 to 11.30
Sat 12 to 3, 6 to 11
ACCESS
£

Good for: *Plaice, complaining about your agent*
Caveats: *No bookings*

Chip shops it must be said ain't glamorous, but somehow Geales has become the Langan's of the frying time world. So you might actually see someone famous here or at the very least sit next to someone who knows someone famous. This is one of the few places where the haddock scented air is thick with words like 'development deal', 'Channel 4' and 'my agent'. None of which obscures the fact that this thoroughly honest and distinctly untrendy place will cheaply and swiftly give you some of London's best fish and chips. Decor has more than a hint of the seaside teashop: chairs are hard, floor is lino, walls are gloss buttercup. The little shaded wall sconces and the frightful tapestry-look drapes are a nod towards gentility. There are briny pictures of fish, fishermen and fishwives on the walls.

The menu – displayed on a wooden board – doesn't muck about: the heart of the matter is still plaice, cod, haddock, rock, lemon sole and dover sole with a few exotic visitors like clams and shark. First courses are minimal – crab soup, fish soup – as are accompaniments. You really come here to eat huge, perfectly fried helpings of fish and chips. You might want to kick off though with a plate of fried clams – virtually the staple food of coastal New

England – shared between two. Reassuringly they run out of things quickly here so you know that if it's not fresh it's not on and they have maintained remarkably high standards. The plaice is always an exemplary fish here rather than the dull little number it often seems. There are vinegar bottles on the tables, but more refined (or perhaps just effete) tastes are catered for with tartar sauce. You might want to liven things up with a gherkin – portentously large and ugly – or some over-enthusiastically dressed coleslaw. In twelve years I've never eaten a pudding here. It gets frightfully crowded: you may have to wait perched on a diminutive stool at the upstairs bar and you may have to share a table as well. The upstairs dining room is dull and *outré*: cognoscenti wait for a seat in the noisy and crowded downstairs. The wine list is surprisingly good with cheap champagne – guzzled enthusiastically by gangs of young hoorays celebrating birthdays – and excellent giveaway (£3.45 a bottle) house white. Hand driers in the loos are manufactured by the firm of Haddock and Horstman, I kid you not.

The George and Vulture

3 Castle Court,
London EC3
Tel: 01-626 9710
Mon-Fri 12 to 2.45
ACCESS, AMEX, DINERS, VISA
£

Good for: *English grills, boisterous lunching*
Caveats: *Meat eaters only*

This is one of the jollier and cheaper places to eat in the
City and probably one of the most interesting members of
the rather homogenised Trusthouse Forte family. It is
tucked away in a labyrinthine alley behind the Royal Ex-
change and cheek by jowl with the Jamaica, the noisiest,
most crowded and one of the oldest public houses in the
City. Not that this place itself is a newcomer: the menu lays
claim to a 1600 birthday and there is a thick enough
veneer of history here to satisfy even the most demanding
American visitor. The decor is chophouse basic with lino
floors, winding staircases, impossibly thick cream paintwork and a parade of coathooks reminiscent of school and
barracks. There are a few judiciously placed prints of 'Pick-
wickian' nature. Seating is communal in stiff wainscoted
booths for five. The table settings are rudimentary: white
linen, canteen grade crockery, standard issue wine glasses
and mustard pots.

The menu doesn't muck about. First courses are English
basic: prawn cocktail, soup, melon, potted shrimps – all
okay and ultra utilitarian. Main courses are scarcely more
inventive, based on the arts of roasting and grilling as
practised by the properly betoqued chef whose kitchen is
virtually in the dining room. Loin and chump chops; rump,

fillet, sirloin and T-bone steaks are good quality, cooked as ordered and plainly dished up. You can have decent chips or sautéed potatoes, perfunctory salads and splendid fried onion rings. Puddings are nurseryesque – coffee okay. The short wine list is slightly cagey about vintages. Service is swift but kindly. Your next-door neighbours will most likely be boys in pinstripes discussing 'markets.'

Gran Paradiso

52 Wilton Road,
London SW1
Tel: 01-828 5818
Mon-Fri 12 to 2.30, 6 to 11.15
Sat 6 to 11.15
ACCESS, AMEX, DINERS, VISA
££

Good for: *Informal power lunches, family dinners*
Caveats: *Menu booby-trapped with clichés*

Wilton Road is the main restaurant drag of otherwise underfed Victoria: there's a cluster of Greek, Italian and Chinese (like Hoizin, *q.v.*) which are for the most part 'useful' rather than particularly interesting. The food at this trat isn't going to set the world alight but there are enough good intentions and sound cooking here to make this place worth visiting more often than just when you happen to be in the neighbourhood. It has a lot of regulars and a surprising number of them seem to be high-powered business and political folk. The feel of the dining room is I suppose *nostalgie de la chasse*; the walls are hung with superannuated rifles, crossbows and misty paintings of wild

Italian landscapes. A stuffed stag's head surveys the clientele. In good post-terrazza-trat style there is a tile floor, white painted brick walls, bentwood chairs and round tables neatly lit by slick dangling spotlights.

The menu is a concise mix of the interesting and banal (yes, there is chicken Kiev) with plats du jour written in a right-hand column. The clichés are well executed using good ingredients but you will be better off following a few of the more innovative hints. So, to begin with, you can have Parma ham with melon or mozzarella, avocado and tomato salad, although the real treat is often something like sautéed chicken livers in rich Madeira sauce. In the summer they do an excellent salad of cold cooked vegetables. There are only a handful of pasta dishes listed on the menu, but the kitchen seems to oblige special requests: I've had excellent spaghetti with tomato and chilli sauce. Fish is limited to sole and salmon, which is always in good condition and well cooked and sometimes they have cut-price lobster. Italian mainstays like a heroic veal chop with garlic and rosemary or T-bone steak are worth having and the chef is particularly good with game. Vegetables are usually up to scratch, although the selection of the day (served of course from those little oval metal dishes) can be over-tired and over-buttered. Pudding is the usual Italian farrago; the espresso is savage. There are some good bottles on the wine list: house wine does the trick for unspecial occasions. Service is brisk.

Green's

36 Duke Street,
London SW1
Tel: 01-930 4566
Mon-Fri 12.30 to 3, 6.30 to 10.30
ACCESS, AMEX, DINERS, VISA
££

> Good for: *High-class snacks, nostalgie de la nursery*
> Caveats: *Careless vegetables*

It is all rather gentlemanly and clublike here and Green's has perhaps surpassed Wilton's – the restaurant which inspired it – as St James's chief public purveyor of fogey-esque fodder. You enter through a small panelled bar with a labyrinth of banquetted nooks: a good place to sit and drink one or two bottles of champagne in the company of the Old Masters dealers who use this as their local watering hole. There are high-class sandwiches and snacks (e.g. quails' eggs) to help soak up the fizz. The next-door dining room is bigger and brighter. There is more polished wood panelling and neatly ragged pale yellow walls hung with piscabilia and evocative pictures such as William Nicholson's stern portrait of Queen Victoria. Table settings are unfussy and correct.

The gloriously unwieldy menu of past days is gone but the new compact version still sports a splendid Jak cartoon of sozzled nobs. Food is of the no-nonsense school: oysters, smoked salmon, cod's roe pâté, cold roast beef. The oysters are gloriously fresh and tangy – among the best in London. Dressed crab makes a pretty zippy first course as well. The plutocratic might kick off with cold boiled lobster – immensely expensive but one of London's top crustaceans. Main courses which owe more to shopping than to cooking –

bangers and mash, smoked turkey, grilled dover sole – will certainly satisfy you without causing undue excitement. The venison hash is comforting and the game – teal, pheasant, partridge – is well cooked and served when it's around. The by now celebrated fishcakes and salmon fishcakes are, alas, a crashing bore – over-stodged and under-flavoured. Vegetables are anonymous with the honourable exception of the doorstep-sized chips. Puddings are old fashioned, good and usually unnecessary. Service from white-jacketed waiters – who may turn out to be francophone Spaniards – is brisk. The wine list is good with some stratospheric prices and the modernistic perspex coolers jar more than a little with the trad decor. Single diners may perch at the bar which often groans under a heap of cooked lobsters like some Flemish still life. There is a gloomy and under-used downstairs dining room.

Grill St Quentin

136 Brompton Road,
London SW3
Tel: 01-581 8377
Mon–Sat 12 to 3, 7 to 11.30
Sun 12 to 3, 7 to 11
ACCESS, AMEX, DINERS, VISA
££

> Good for: *Sunday nights, steak and chips*
> Caveats: *Steer clear of tinnies*

This less formal (and cheaper) cousin to the St Quentin across the road admirably sets out to present a short, simple menu in agreeably casual surroundings, and it does it well most of the time. If you enter from Brompton Road you might make a last-minute decision to duck into the Thai restaurant next door (they share an awning): if you don't it's down the stairs, through an agreeable parquet-floored wine bar, past a brace of charcoal grills and into the main dining room. Come in from Cheval Place and you get to the room through a small shop selling upmarket tinned food (more about that in a minute). The dining room is pleasantly Froggy – tiled floor, claret-coloured banquettes, expensive fittings.

First courses may be oeuf en gelée, mediocre rillettes de saumon or various pâtés and terrines. The previously foie gras shy will be relieved to know that the fowl are 'forcibly fed by a method which they do not appear to resent' – go tell Mother Goose that. Main courses are mostly grills: usually decent steaks, lamb chops or brochette of lotte, all well accompanied by huge helpings of chips, not necessarily the best chips you've ever tasted, but well above average. There are plats du jour, too, like veal marengo. The rot, alas, sets in with the section entitled 'by Comtesse du Barry', a selection of confit du canard, cassoulet or cous-cous decanted from the fancy tins on sale next door and served up in the restaurant. There's no moral dilemma about a restaurant serving tinned food, but in this case marketing (you'll taste here and be so impressed that you'll buy a case on the way out) seems to have triumphed over common sense. Who is going into a restaurant to order something knowing that le chef will merely get out le tin opener? Surely this bravely foolish experiment has gone on for too long and mars an otherwise sensible and useful establishment. Puddings are excellent. Service from largely monolingual (French only) staff is sometimes puzzled, but gets the job done.

Heals

196 Tottenham Court Road,
London W1
Tel: 01-631 1921
Mon-Sat 10 to 5.30
(Thurs until 7)
ACCESS, AMEX, DINERS, VISA
££

> Good for: *Breakfast, stews*
> Caveats: *Confusingly multinational lunches*

Along with L'Express (*q.v.*) this must be the best restaurant in a shop in London: good enough to attract more than just the captive audience of the carrier-bag laden. Unsurprising, considering the restaurateur background of Sir Terence Conran. Directors of the Conran empire may be seen munching here, along with chic young householders and boys and girls who wear plastic spectacles and black sneakers and carry rolled-up copies of *Blueprint*. Befitting the Heals context it is more well designed than Designer, but there are just enough 'references' to keep the cognoscenti happy. So the wooden screens which subdivide the room hint at the Viennese secession and the wooden furniture evokes the style of Ambrose Heal. The comfortable banquettes are upholstered in dark green bird's-eye. It is all rather spacious and simple and quiet without being hushed.

The menu is short and trendily eclectic inclining towards the sort of high-class peasant food that architects currently favour: there are things like grilled goat's cheese with marjoram, for example, and the yoghurt is Greek, of course. The cooking is in fact far better than its around-the-world-in-a-dinner-party menu suggests. Crostini – those excellent

Italian rounds of grilled bread smeared with various savouries – are forceful and honest. Basque pipérade – an open-faced omelette with tomatoes, peppers and ham – was warming and good. There is a dab hand in the kitchen with stews and it's sad that so few other restaurants bother to do them properly. Lamb stew with olives and yellow rice filled a hole rather deftly. The fish here is expensive but good and often appears in frightfully smart guise. Fillets of St Pierre (along with brill, the designer fish of the moment) with asparagus and chervil was delicate and perfectly cooked. Salads and vegetables are first rate. Puddings (like apple tart with lashings of double cream) are rich and comforting. Coffee is pukka. You can have breakfast here if you like or afternoon tea: there are newspapers to read. On late-night shopping day (Thursday) they have a happy hour, so you can prop up the bar and sip punt e mes while debating the future of post-modernist interior decoration. Service is youthful, cheery and efficient in the American fashion. Maybe they should be open for dinner as well.

Hiders

755 Fulham Road,
London SW6
Tel: 01-736 2331
Mon-Fri 12.30 to 2.30, 7.30 to 11.30
ACCESS, AMEX, VISA
££

> Good for: *Intimate celebrations, pigeon*
> Caveats: *Easy to fall off chairs near front door*

In an astonishingly short time, Hiders has established itself as the grand restaurant for that quarter of Southwest London that is now chockablock with City Johnnies, young married Sloane couples and what marketing men call 20—35-year-old ABs, namely the most upwardly mobile part of the restaurant-going population. What owner Richard Griggs and chef Paul Duvall have accomplished lies largely in providing what I suppose is generally considered 'West End' cooking and atmosphere at knock-downish prices. Decor is plush without intimidation: a rather severe lack of windows is disguised by a large mirror population swagged in velvet drapes. The ground floor has both a chandelier and a mahogany bar (for serving rather than for hanging about) and a few banquettes; downstairs has (in the winter) a roaring gas fire, which is jolly welcome on wintry nights even if it might render your lamb's kidneys bien cuit rather than pink. There is proper nappery and hefty wine glasses. A plate of amuse-gueules – usually little bits of barbequed chicken and warm cheese-filled pastry puffs – hits the table as soon as you do.

The short menu changes frequently and describes the cooking in vocabulary that seems to borrow equally from Oscar Wilde and Syrie Maugham; it certainly leaves little to

75

the imagination. 'Médaillons of veal set on a rich périgour-
dine sauce, garnished with truffles and a broccoli mousse'
is pretty self-explanatory. In the last year some of the
baroque excesses of the language and the cookery have
been toned down and this kitchen now consistently turns
out top whack imaginative food. When loony invention
manifests itself, it's usually in the form of some avoidable
soup like apple and fennel (no kidding). First courses may
be of the mousse/feuilleté/salad school or sometimes more
elaborate like a salmon and chive sausage. The salads are
always delicious and perhaps vital if you're proceeding to a
pudding. Complex sounding main courses like 'breast of
chicken coated in lemon, parmesan and breadcrumbs and
placed on a shallot sauce garnished with bacon and button
onions' are simpler and jazzier tasting than they sound.
Pigeon is invariably excellent, lamb is beautifully cooked
and the fish (usually only one on offer) is first rate though
sometimes overwrought. Vegetables – regrettably served
in a little 'selection' – are well cooked. Puddings are rich,
hard to resist and verging on the immoral. There is a short
wine list printed down one side of the menu: house wines
are well chosen, but they could do with a few more down-
market clarets. Service by waiters of interesting though
indeterminate nationality is courteous and efficient. It is
one of the more enjoyable restaurants in town, hence it is
always packed. Lunch is quieter and cheaper. The name,
incidentally, comes from a farmhouse that was in the
owner's family.

Hilaire

68 Old Brompton Road,
London SW7
Tel: 01-584 8993
Mon-Fri 12.30 to 2.30, 7 to 11.30
Sat 7 to 11.30
ACCESS, AMEX, DINERS, VISA
££

> Good for: *Impressing gastronomes, celebratory lunches*
> Caveats: *Pricey wine*

This review is more about Simon Hopkinson than his restaurant. Alongside Alistair Little (*q.v.*), Hopkinson is at the very least the best young chef in London. At the end of this year (1987) he moves from this tiny Kennedy Brookes owned establishment to his own restaurant in the newly restored Conran-backed Michelin Building just down the road. His new place is going to be called Bibendum after the nail-drinking Michelin mascot. In an earlier incarnation Hilaire was a burger joint called Brookes. Physically not much has changed, but the cosmetics are more upmarket. The walls are painted sage and hung with nineteenth-century landscapes. The table settings are awfully proper with trencherman intention: stiff white nappery, heavy cutlery and vast simple wine glasses. Two tables in bay windows jut out onto Old Brompton Road (South Kensington High Street) and in the small basement there's a pair of tables set in barrel-vaulted alcoves.

Hopkinson has rather deftly learned a lot of the lessons of the new cookery without ever resorting to pretension or trickery. The food here is inventive, gutsy and distinguished: not a place where you chase a radicchio leaf around a big octagonal plate. This is one of the few restaurants in London where you can find that same lusty elemental love of food that characterises some of the great French restaurants. You might begin with something like a wobbly tower of warm spinach mousse served with the most perfect mustardy flavoured hollandaise you can imagine or a splendid teaming of herring and gravadlax with a dill and horseradish mousse. Hopkinson's fish cookery approaches the orgasmic: fillets of red mullet with basil on a bed (I did say orgasmic) of green tagliatelle was utterly sensational. Things like steak au poivre – which might have started out as a fairly jokey concession to mainstream taste – or fillet of veal with fresh ceps are cooked in a way which is both muscular and sensitive. Vegetables are perfectly cooked. I usually can't get through the pudding stage here but the Christmas pudding ice cream was one of the treats of the year. There is a fairly cheap set lunch too. Customers are *bon ton*, the atmosphere is serious without being grave and the service is youthful but proper. There's not much to drink for under £10.00.

Hoizin

72/73 Wilton Road,
London SW1
Tel: 01-630 5108
Mon–Sat 12 to 2.30, 6 to 11.30
ACCESS, AMEX, VISA
££

Good for: *Vegetarians, modernists, scallops*   Caveats: *Piped music*

First slop, then glop, then hot, then not – a good mnemonic for tracing the rise of Chinese cooking in this country from cynical to over-sauced, over-MSGed vaguely Cantonese to

78

throat-burning Szechuanish to a more modern lighter and purer style of cooking. ZenW3 (*q.v.*) practises it and so does Hoizin, honourable purveyor of 'Chinese seafood cuisine'. There is a small cocktail bar at the entrance and, more notably, a chilled display of fish and somnolent lobsters waiting for the pot or griddle. The upstairs dining room – there is a larger and, I think, rather more anonymous room downstairs – is long and narrow with a picture window giving views of Wilton Road punters scurrying to one or other of the restaurants now booming in the neighbourhood. The look is neo-Chinese minimalist: white walls decorated with huge calligraphic prints. (One, a poem, describes drunkenness as ascending a pagoda – fall from the top floor included, I assume.) The wall sconces are shaped like seashells. Tables are set with severity, although your chopstick rest may be a ceramic tiger, chicken or bunny.

The menu as in most Chinese restaurants is long but thankfully unnumbered. Fishy dishes preponderate: four sorts of lobster, eight different prawn dishes, three different eels. First courses excel, although they will prepare boring old sesame prawn toast or crispy – aren'tyajustsickofit – seaweed. Hot poached mixed seafood skewers are a much better idea as are the mussels in black bean sauce and chilli. The deep-fried scallops in a thin batter are melting and good. Main course fish and veg are better than main course meat: the owners also own a Chinese fishmonger in Soho and a farm growing Chinese vegetables in Bedfordshire. The by now statutory aromatic crispy duck is perfectly well prepared, but no better or worse than in most upmarket Chinese places. Sizzling lamb is glutinous and dull. The seafood is superb: grilled fish (usually sea bass or dover sole) irreproachable, the Chinese broccoli with crabmeat good news. Vegetables like asparagas and straw mushrooms or dry-fried French beans are well prepared as are the noodles with bean sprouts. The service is friendly and helpful; the piped music – 'My Way', 'Nights in White Satin' – simply dreadful.

Hollywood's

2 Hollywood Road,
London SW10
Tel: 01-352 6884
Mon-Sat 12.30 to 3, 7.30 to 11
Sun 12.30 to 2.30, 7.30 to 10.30
ACCESS, AMEX, DINERS, VISA
££

Good for: *Hip brochettes, Saturday lunch*
Caveats: *Wear sunglasses*

Hollywood Road is the Greek Street of Sloanesville, chockablock with restaurants and double parked with Golf GTIs and BMWs. The good, the bad and the indifferent co-exist and seem to thrive here. The venerable Chinese bistro, the Golden Duck, is the senior statesman; this place is most definitely the new kid on the block, presenting a pretty glitzy and self-assured front to the world from its corner site. It has a most respectable provenance – the manager Patrice Mossadek ran the restaurant at Blakes Hotel splendidly (*q.v.*) for many years and his new operation has some of the same sleek sexiness and eclectic cookery as Blakes. Rigged out in dazzling white and the soft clear light of those frightfully expensive Italian light fixtures, the ground floor brasserie makes you feel as if you've arrived for a pyjama party at the villa of some North African plutocrat. There's a bar and a rear dining room overlooking a garden terrace.

The menu here is hip and global, ranging from bouillabaisse and *au courant* lukewarm salads to raclette and some pretty gutsy brochettes. Down the staircase is where the action really is though, in the chic and slightly naughty basement dining room. The marble floor is splendid, the linen stiff, the chairs comfortable, the glasses big and the frightfully chic Christofle cutlery ought to be chained to the table. The menu is brief and perhaps somewhat over-fanciful. You might begin with vegetables chausson: a little puff pastry case filled with neatly cooked vegetables and a glob of Hollandaise suffering, alas, from the dumb blonde syndrome (good looking, dull tasting) or a well-thought-out warm salad of quail and artichoke. I hope that scallops in rose water and chervil is better than it sounds. Main courses like beef with hazelnuts or liver with Meaux mustard are less fey than they appear, but perhaps a little lacking in brio. A *la* Blakes they do proper wild rice and a fairly serious potato gratin. Puddings – ice cream, fruit crepes, iced fruit pavé – are best shared. There is a good range of tea and coffee. The wine list if short and not overladen with bargains, but the house wines are first rate. Service may err towards the sombre. Fellow diners dress up: wear your Yohji Yamamoto and Vuitton tote bag.

Ikeda

30 Brook Street,
London W1
Tel: 01-629 2730
Mon-Fri 12.30 to 2.30, 6.30 to 10.30
ACCESS, AMEX, DINERS, VISA
£££

Good for: *Raw tuna, respite from shopping*
Caveats: *Ring bank manager first*

London's Japanese restaurants can be a bit depressing: the grim hygiene, the uncommunicative staff, the tiresome litany of a handful of familiar dishes. I must say that I find this place, along with the much scruffier Ikkyu (*q.v.*), the most agreeable and interesting Japanese restaurant in London. Even though it sits in the luxurious purlieus of South Molton Street it is still a bit spartan. You duck under a succession of hanging blue clothes emblazoned with ideograms presumably extolling the virtues of the chef, the freshness of the fish, the fragrance of the waitresses and so on. There is a small semi-circular lino-clad bar where a posse of Japanese box wallahs perch, engaged in the serious business of getting regless on Chivas Regal. The rear dining room is small and too brightly lit. The walls are rough plastered, the banquettes black upholstered and inconceivably upright, the tables veneered in plastic wood.

The menu is a treat, full of esoterica (salted cuttlefish guts) and adventure (sashimi is 'sliced rapidly with a dangerously sharp knife'). First courses are small and perfectly formed: cold spinach with soy sauce or brinily fresh salmon roe on a little mound of grated white radish. The sushi (shrimp, salmon, mackerel, cuttlefish) is splendid, the tuna sashimi quite unbelievably wonderful. Standard dishes like

82

tempura are flawlessly executed with top-class ingredients and the presentation is simple and bold. Fish is well cooked, particularly the salt grilled turbot. My favourite vegetable is the creamy grilled aubergine with sesame seeds. Pudding is fruit neatly dissected and prettily presented. You will probably want to drink either sake or the icy Japanese beer. The toothpicks are a marvel of woodturning. Prices are, of course, astronomical.

Ikkyu

---

67 Tottenham Court Road,
London W1
Tel: 01-636 9280
Mon-Fri 12.30 to 2.30, 6 to 11
Sun 6 to 11
ACCESS, AMEX, DINERS, VISA
£

> Good for: *After hi-fi shopping, cheap sushi*
> Caveats: *Leave party frock at home*

It must be the most modest and in many ways the most enjoyable Japanese restaurant in London, a far cry indeed from the expense-account-floated West End heavies like Suntory (*q.v.*). Ikkyu's basement dining room is one full step up from transport café status and a flight of steps below a typical Tottenham Road hi-fi shop appropriately flogging the products of Rising Sun Imperialism. Decor and furnishings are more basic than minimalist; the sheer stylessness of the surroundings are part of the charm of this place. The tables are covered in plastic laminate, the floor is lino, the seating is on leatherette banquette or creaky cesca chair. A kite hangs from the ceiling, a few prints hang on the wall: there are crates and crates of lager (Kirin and Kestrel in a bicultural gesture) and bottles of Bell's.

The menu is homely and interesting with more unusual dishes than your average Japanese. It offers amongst other fish 'glilled pike', I kid you not. The sushi is plentiful and good – mackerel, octopus, cuttlefish, salmon – nicely presented on a dish shaped like a little wooden platform and thankfully lacking the over-decoration that plagues so much Japanese food. Instead of tempura you may want to try their fried prawns: a brace of brutes crisply and drily fried in a rough crunchy batter served with what tasted like plum sauce. The 'glilled' fish are marvellous – grilled herring was black and crispy on the outside, succulent and perfectly cooked on the inside. Garnishes (half an orange with the prawns) can be a bit weird. The soy bean paste soup which accompanies all the set meals is hearty and delicious – a cut above the usual. Puddings are rudimentary: fresh fruit only. (The sweet-of-tooth can wander a few doors away to Bernigra, stellar makers and sellers of Italian ice cream.) You can drink warm and potent sake from little porcelain carafes or cold lager. Service from charming and mostly monolingual young Japanese women is swift but rather puzzled. Solitary diners or those with an excess of street cred will want to sit at the bar. Most unJapanesely, helpings are ample. Japanese folk music plinks, boings and wavers in the background.

Joe Allen

13 Exeter Street,
London WC2
Tel: 01–836 0651
Mon–Sat 12 to 1 am
Sun 12 to 12
NO CREDIT CARDS
£

> Good for: *Late-night fodder, children*
> Caveats: *Extremely rude*

There are only a few passable restaurants in Covent Garden and not even a few decent American restaurants in all
of London, so this place, in spite of its glaring shortcomings,
has a lot going for it. To begin with it looks and feels like a
decent New York bar with parquet floors, a long dark wood
bar, round tables with checked tablecloths and unpainted
brick walls hung with a profusion of theatrical memorabilia
– black-and-white photos of the now or once famous and
posters advertising long-gone West End shows. The waiters
– in white shirts and long aprons – bustle, the clientele
looks pretty good.

There is no printed menu, just a lengthy blackboarded
roll call of American specialities: chilli, ribs, hamburgers
(sorry, chopped steak), eggs benedict, grilled chicken – all
good sloppy uncomplicated dishes. The paper napkins and
the bottle of ketchup on each table signal good basic eating
too. Something has gone wrong between the concept and
the kitchen though. The once celebrated black bean soup
looks up to scratch, but tastes of nothing and may arrive
tepid instead of hot. The chopped liver is okay even if it
wouldn't rate much applause off Broadway. Some of the
trademark main courses like Eggs Joe Allen – poached egg

and spinach in a potato skin – are tasty enough but much of
the cooking and assembly is, to be kind, rather lacklustre.
Even the salads taste like production line products. Puddings are good, gooey and calorific – banana cream pie,
chocolate mousse pie, carrot cake, brownies. Somewhere
along the line the heart has gone out of this restaurant.
They certainly don't go out of their way to make you feel
welcome. When booking you may be asked to give your
table up at a certain time; service is often grudging and

APICELLA '86

impatient, bills arrive unasked for. I can't help feeling that the sheer gracelessness of this establishment is the product of the sort of cynical attitude that sees customers as 'throughput' rather than guests. Still it is immensely successful, remarkably cheap and a decent place to take children. And they have the excellent Rolling Rock Beer, that most distinguished product of Latrobe, Pennsylvania.

Julie's

135 Portland Road,
London W11
Tel: 01–727 4585
Mon–Sat 12.30 to 2.15, 7.30 to 11.15
Sun 12.30 to 2.15, 7.30 to 10.30
ACCESS, AMEX, DINERS, VISA
££

Good for: *Sunday lunch, homely eating*
Caveats: *Some fanciful dinner party food*

The years have given a patina of respectability to this once
louche hangout of the beautiful people. Many of the clientele seemed to have aged *in situ*, forever frozen into a
champagne-clutching sprawl on one of the sofas by the
fireplace in the bar. You pass through a prettily pale
ground-floor bar to wind down the stairs to where the
action really is. The bar has enough nooks and crannies to
have the smell of sexual intrigue in the air. The dining
room itself is whitewashed, catacombish and candle lit.
The tables are neatly dressed in pink nappery.

The menu is longish and sometimes looks like a pro-
gramme for one of those enlightened dinner parties given
by *Guardian* readers. So you'll find some bravely adventurous but jolly silly dishes on it like calves' liver with
blueberries or baked mullet with fennel purée. But there
are good and sensible things too. You might begin with
spicy chicken livers with scrambled eggs or a comforting
soup like lentil and ham. Some dishes that require more
than a modicum of technique aren't particularly well executed. A watercress mousse was strangled with cream and
gelatine: vegetable terrine looked good but tasted rather
pointless. Meaty main courses are best. Steak and kidney

pie is big and heartening; things like steaks and rack of lamb are well cooked and generously presented. Vegetables are homely – parsnips, potato pancakes and so on – and served family style. Puddings are traditional and usually *de trop*. Obliging service is provided by members of the latest generation of pretty, trendy girls. The wine list is okay; the neighbouring antique shops worth looking in. Sunday lunch is an institution here, as are aristocratic stag parties in the private room.

Kalamaras (Mega)

76–78 Inverness Mews,
London W2
Tel: 01-727 9122
Mon–Sat 7 pm to midnight
ACCESS, AMEX, DINERS, VISA
£

> Good for: *Seduction, upmarket vegetarians*
> Caveats: *Mornings after excess retsina*

Greek food is, alas, not universally admired. It is – they say – a) oily, b) boring and c) even worse in Greece than it is here. London is of course chockablock with local kebab houses mostly, I must admit, a) oily, b) boring and c) better than in Greece. Even so I am an unashamed partisan of Greek cooking; know three or four good Greek restaurants in London and steer clear of the run of the mill, usually Greek Cypriot, joints. The only Greek restaurants in London though – *pace* the White Tower (*q.v.*) – with any claim to real culinary distinction are the two Kalamaras, cheek by jowel in a tiny Bayswater cul de sac. Micro is smaller, cheaper, less comfortable, unlicensed and youthful. Mega is the grown-up version. A long low (the tall should avoid being seated along the right-hand wall) dining room stretches from street to open kitchen. Lighting is dim, chairs are rustic, walls sport Greek ethnobilia.

The menu is long, printed in transliterated Greek and hence incomprehensible. So one of the young and enthusiastic waitresses will come to your table and run the gamut thusly: 'Loukanika is spicy Greek sausage, taramasalata is a purée of cod's roe, blah, blah, blah . . .' You listen attentively and try to remember what sounds best: repeat visitors do better. Unless you are a complete bozo of the anal retentive variety – the sort who won't let other people share 'his' dish in a Chinese restaurant – you will go for a mass orgy of first courses and be mighty pleased: the aforementioned tarama and loukanika are superb, as are the artichokes with broad beans, the cheese in puff pastry, the fried aubergines with garlic dip and whatever else you might order. Main courses are good but not quite as sparkling. Nonetheless, the lamb and pork are top quality and forthrightly cooked as kebabs or in stews with lemon or spinach. Fish is the best thing, though, particularly a huge and neatly trimmed selection of mixed fish presented in a filo pastry sack. The Greek salads are compulsively good. There is the usual battery of nutty, sticky puddings. Retsina – the pine dosed hootch that smells like the floor of a busy operating theatre – is the stuff to drink: more timid diners have a decent range of non-resinated Greek to choose from. Very late at night the owner and a few friends pull out bouzouki and guitars and sing sad songs: and jolly nice it is too.

Langan's Bistro

26 Devonshire Street,
London W1
Tel: 01-935 4531
Mon-Fri 12.30 to 2.30, 7 to 11.30
Sat 7 to 11.30
AMEX
££

> Good for: *First dates, after Harley Street*
> Caveats: *Some tables for two uncomfortable*

If you walk here by way of Westmoreland Street you pass a blue plaque marking the erstwhile home of the eighteenth-century divine and hymnist Charles Wesley; alas the site is now a public house. Sober speculation cannot predict the future occupants of 26 Devonshire Street where the acorn which blossomed into Peter Langan's gastronomic oaks (viz. Odins, Langan's Brasserie, both *q.v.*, Peter Langan's Bar and Grill) was first planted. Indeed, in days gone by, Peter Langan actually cooked here. Today this place is, I suppose, the most modest member of the Langan restaurant family. In Langan hallmark fashion the walls are closely hung with pictures: a still life of a boiled lobster with flowers, photos of Peter Langan leaning on a Bentley bumper and a young co-respondent-shoed David Hockney drinking al fresco. Upside-down parasols adorn the ceiling; a leather rhinoceros surveys the front door. The side chairs and banquettes are upholstered in dowdy plushtex.

The broadsheet-sized menu features a Patrick Proctor study of Langan contemplating the mysteries of a glass of white wine. In the same glorious purple script favoured by other Langan establishments the menu offers a brief and sometimes intriguing selection. There is a bizarre, but satisfying marriage of creamy goat's cheese with pickled pears or maybe a happily unballasty gratin of mixed fish or some *au courant* salad like chicory and bacon. Main courses are cooked with care if without inspiration. So the escalope of salmon in tarragon sauce arrives in a similar creamy pool to the breast of chicken with wild mushrooms. A selection of vegetables – neatly cooked – turns up in a little oval dish. Mrs Langan's chocolate pudding is by now the most famous glob of calories in the metropolis, but other puddings like strawberry syllabub are good for the piggy too. There is a decent wine list. Service is youthful.

Langan's Brasserie

Stratton Street,
London W1
Tel: 01-491 8822
Mon–Fri 12.30 to 2.45, 7 to 11.45
Sat 8 pm to 12.45 am
ACCESS, AMEX, DINERS, VISA
££

> Good for: *Honest food, serious celebrating*
> Caveats: *Book in advance*

This place is as much a phenomenon as a restaurant. After ten years it remains fashionable and exciting, a restaurant where lunch or dinner is an occasion. There may be fewer stars here than in the early days and perhaps more suburban spivs, bimbos and tourists, but Langan's remains a restaurant where celebrities and the uncelebrated co-exist in perfect comfort. More than any other London restaurant it has the verve and cachet of the great Parisian brasseries.

The decor has aged well: the dragged walls, upholstery of indeterminate colour and the fabulous pictures make as splendid a setting as ever. Waiters in black waistcoats, white shirts and long aprons wait attentively. Look at the table settings – paper tablecloths, utilitarian cutlery, ice buckets on the table – and you can see quite clearly that this is not the sort of place where you toy with the dill sprig garnish on a big octagonal plate: this establishment is for proper eating and drinking.

The menu – still thankfully headed by David Hockney's delightful portrait of owners Peter Langan, Richard Shepherd and Michael Caine – is marvellously lengthy: over 100 items. The wonder is that the kitchen turns out so many of diverse meals a day with so few hiccoughs. The canonical first courses are splendid. The spinach soufflé with anchovy sauce or the little croustade filled with mushroom duxelle, quails' eggs and hollandaise are cooked with finesse and served with generosity. The salade frisée is one of the best in London and how many other restaurants still do celery rémoulade. Soups – like purée of lentil – are good and rustic. Main courses are big, bold and direct. Tongue with Madeira sauce, boeuf bourguignon with mashed potatoes, roast chicken are all the real thing. Escalope de veau is a heroic helping. Fish – including my favourite goujons de lotte – is respectfully cooked. Vegetables are good and interesting; the bubble and squeak a dream; salads perfunctory. The pudding list inclines towards the Froggy with excellent fruit tartes. The wine list – printed on the right hand side of the menu – is concise; house wine usually does the trick, but the choice of ten champagnes suggests the celebratory status of the place. Service is exemplary though booking is a little difficult. The upstairs Venetian Room with its Patrick Proctor murals is slowly becoming acceptable after years of unfashionability. By anyone's standards – and people do like to take pot shots – this is one of London's greatest restaurants.

Launceston Place Restaurant

1a Launceston Place,
London W8
Tel: 01-937 6912
Mon-Sun 12.30 to 2.30
Mon-Sat 6.30 to 11.30
ACCESS, VISA
££

> Good for: *Well-bred ambience, bubble and squeak*
> Caveats: *Too many oranges*

Simon Slater and Nick Smallwood are savvy operators. They both rose to prominence at the Zanzibar, soothing the egos and lightening the chequebooks of London trendies: Slater stayed for a while, Smallwood went off to contribute mightily to the success of L'Escargot (*q.v.*). Last year they got together to open up their own restaurant on the site of what used to be a neighbourhood favourite, the Casa Porelli, in one of Kensington's most picturesque and pricey neighbourhoods. These days, when the cult of the chef is perhaps at its height, we tend to forget just how much management and so called 'front-of-house' ability contribute to any restaurant: there seem to be sadly few young restaurateurs of ability and Slater and Smallwood are certainly most able and energetic. This surprisingly rambling little restaurant has been rather sprucely done up like a smart hotel – there are some nice Edwardian pictures.

The cooking is essentially what I suppose is now called 'modern British', well mannered and just on the conservative side of trendy. The kitchen may have its lapses when inventiveness gets the better of good sense – I remember salmon with blood orange sauce – but you will eat well here. First courses include a preponderance of the raw, the cosmopolitan and the salad-like. You may have marinated raw fish or gumbo (the soups here are very good). There are always a couple of traditional main courses for irredeemable young fogeys – roast lamb and the inevitable steak – but the more adventurous will be well rewarded. The fish is usually first rate and is sensitively handled and the far too often boring old breast of chicken is tasty and succulent in its various guises. Vegetables are okay – the bubble and squeak heroic. Puddings are rich and reminiscent of half-timbered cottages and ads for the British Tourist Authority (e.g. apple and blueberry crumble with clotted cream); cheeses – as is the new fashion – are farmhouse, obscure and excellent. The wine list is shortish, comprehensive enough and not unfairly priced. Their Sunday lunch has rapidly become celebrated. Confident, unruffled and not too cruel on the budget, it is a favoured hangout for yuppie sloanies – do park the Range Rover around the corner though.

Leek's Fish Bar

23 Lavender Hill,
London SW11
Tel: 01-228 9460
Mon–Sat 11.30 to 2.30, 5 to 10.30
ACCESS, AMEX, DINERS, VISA
£

> Good for: *Saturday lunch, low key celebrations,*
> *indetectable trysts*
> Caveats: *Chips too good for slimmers*

This may not be the best chip shop in London: it is probably (with Geales, *q.v.*) the most agreeable. Indeed chip shop isn't quite the right word as Leek's occupies what should be the increasingly desirable middle ground between the corner chippie – utilitarian dispenser of haddock, saveloys and chips – and a proper fish restaurant. It is a not unsuitable adornment to the heavily restauranted area around the junction of Queenstown Road and Lavender Hill. This dining room could almost be by the seaside: decorative frou frous are kept to a decent minimum. So there is a tiled floor, straight-backed (and hard-bottomed) wooden chairs, oilskin tablecloths (albeit with a jocular print) and functional table settings featuring a bottle of malt vinegar and a squidgy red plastic ketchup 'dispenser'. Bar arrangements are minimal too: a glass-fronted fridge full of white wine, Becks beer and Perrier. Fishy watercolours look down from the walls.

First courses are, let's say, unelaborate: fish soup, melon, prawn cocktail or juicy fried mushrooms served abundantly in an ichthyoid glass dish with an unsubtle garlic mayonnaise. Fish is served either fried or steamed. Cod, haddock, plaice, halibut, rock and skate are usually on offer. Or you might want a brace of Moby-Dick-sized fish-cakes. The frying is crisp and precise and the steaming shows some real sensitivity in the kitchen. Accompaniments are rudimentary: fat, well-bronzed chips, steamed new potatoes, mushy peas or pickled cucumbers. There are slightly fancier dishes of the day like steamed sea bream with cream and mushrooms. Puddings are generous, old fashioned and home made. Coffee is strong and serviceable. The house white is worthy of any fish restaurant: sharpish, cheapish and cold. Clientele – newly transpontine Sloane Rangers, old regulars in for chicken and chips, local businessmen – is egalitarian and unpompous. Service is informal, cheerful and ultra-efficient. It is altogether an excellent example of a better-than-neighbour-hood restaurant accomplishing its limited aims swiftly and superbly with no fuss, pretension or bother: if only there were more like it. They do takeaways as well for the VCRless.

Ley-Ons

56 Wardour Street,
London W1
Tel: 01-437 6465
Mon-Sun 11.30 to 11.15
ACCESS, AMEX, DINERS, VISA
£

Good for: *Late lunches, paper-wrapped chicken*
Caveats: *Watch out for ducks' feet*

You are addressed in print here by the chap who wrote the menu as 'my friend'. And 'my friend' the menu writing mandarin counsels 'for those of you who have to look after your waistlines do not despair. Cantonese cuisine is not fattening. Look around and tell me if you have ever seen a fat Chinese gentleman or lady'. Well, my friend, I have, but I don't remember their names. In spite of the coy prose, this is an establishment of some antiquity (est. 1926) and no little grandeur: there is a vast acreage of marble panelling (in browns, greens and pinks) left over from some earlier incarnation and large murals of edible wildlife. A recent redecoration has given the place a touch of Fu Manchu post-modernism – there is a screen of green, red and gold, Chinese columns, mega-smart light fixtures and futuristic aluminium handrails, but the marvellously tatty red leatherette chairs remain.

The menu is rambling and not dissimilar to many of the other nearby Cantonese restaurants. The brave can snack on yam croquettes or spicy ducks' feet, a dish I find rather pointless. Fortunately for the conservative even the most mundane dishes are well prepared. The dim sum are excellent and cheap – half a dozen selections make a good light lunch for the picky eater. The usual gamut of soups are nicely done, using rather better than average ingredients. Paper-wrapped chicken is crispy, gingery and well presented: spicy brisket of beef is a marvellously comforting cold-weather dish. Vegetables are ungloppy – there are splendid chewy Chinese mushrooms with seasonal vegetables and good Monks mixed vegetables too. The tea is flowery and refreshing. You might want to try a bottle of Greatwall Chinese wine made 'from the Dragon Eye grapes' which is tasty enough but fortunately not the only white wine in the world. In spite of stony greetings at the door, service is obliging. Downstairs there is a large banqueting room which I assume is used for the Chinese equivalent of bar mitzvah parties. This is altogether a correct, slightly old-fashioned Cantonese restaurant and cheap to boot.

About Tables . . .

I arrived in a restaurant for the first time and the maître d' greeted me and scanned the reservation list sedulously. 'Ah, let's see . . . Grossman. Just one moment, Mr Grossman, I just want to be sure to give you a special table.' I smiled and waited. The 'special' table turned out to be under the stairs between the loo door and the fire extinguisher.

So, the more they fuss the more you're being set up to take a dive. Bad tables can be glaringly obvious: in the middle of a room, next to a service area, in a freezing draft with your back to the action. Alas, every restaurant has some 'environmentally' bad tables and as no restaurant is a democracy you, unless you are very rich and famous, are going to get one of them. If you're given an atrocious table ask for another one pronto. If they can't oblige, leave. Otherwise you could be in for a miserable couple of courses.

The socially bad table is more problematical. You may not get Michael Caine's table, but you might want at least the table next to it. If you don't know a restaurant well enough to ask for a specific table you have to brazen it out. Maître d's do look at obvious things like your shoes, haircut and sex/power appeal when doling out tables, although fortunately we're less crippled by table hierarchy than they are in America.

Ma Cuisine

113 Walton Street,
London SW3
Tel: 01-584 7585
Mon-Fri 12.30 to 2, 7.30 to 11
AMEX, DINERS
££

> Good for: *Terrines, treats for gourmets, copper freaks*
> Caveats: *Spaced out service, too-intimate seating*

Whey Guy Mouilleron opened Ma Cuisine in 1975 it was stampeded into the top rank of London's best restaurants: gourmets and the merely fashionable fought for bookings in this tiny restaurant. Alas, the tide of food fashions moved on and Mouilleron's deft and delicious cooking fell from grace. At one time he thought of selling up but thankfully he is still at the stove. The dining room is narrow and uncomfortable (perhaps intimate is a more acceptable description) and decorated with artlessness. One long wall is panelled, one is hessianed, there are still lives of food, an over-abundance of copper pans (including one made into a clock) and a bookcase full of Armagnac. Lucky parties of four may slip into banquettes; twos may suffer unwanted intimacy with their neighbours.

The menu is devoid of pointless neologisms or predictably classic dishes. Terrines – discredited by the inadequacies of second-rate cooks (nothing makes the heart sink more than sole terrine) – are a featured first course and quite rightly. There is fresh and briny fish, a tricoleur of peppers and a mouth-watering partridge terrine laced with carrots and wrapped in cabbage leaves. Mouilleron's famous red mullet soup still has pride of place among the hot first courses and there is a delicious and perhaps too

100

large tarte of buttery pastry filled with leeks and salmon. Main courses are earthy and delicious, displaying a real understanding of food and technique. My favourite is a splendid dish of monkfish and scallops with basil on a bed of thin crispy potaoes. But there are failures too: veal with a seafood tartlet (veal and shellfish go together well) was more a marriage of convenience than a love match. Vegetables are good even if served in a frightfully irritating little selection. The tarte tatin is a hard pudding to resist. Good coffee is served with glacéd fruit. Serious American women clutching Gault-Millau like to lunch here and you might hear someone say, 'when you talk about portfolio risks, blah blah blah'. It is refreshingly unpompous and probably one of the few London restaurants with a straightforward dedication towards good food of the sort you get in better restaurants in France. The wine list is a black mark – far too pricey. Service, sadly, is sans le gorm.

Manzi's

1-2 Leicester Street,
London WC2
Tel: 01-734 0224
Mon-Sat 12 to 2.40, 5.30 to 11.40
Sun 6 to 10.40
ACCESS, AMEX, DINERS, VISA
££

Good for: *Unfussy fish, cheering up*
Caveats: *Listless vegetables*

There are really only two types of restaurant: those that serve braised celery and those that don't. The braised celery lot have old-fashioned food, well-dressed eccentric waiters and an ingenuous comfiness. They are, alas, a dying breed, but a few stalwarts of the braised celery school – like this place – carry on and flourish. Along with Sweetings (*q.v.*) this is London's best traditional fish restaurant. The ground-floor dining room (for reasons unknown the upstairs 'Cabin Room' is unfashionable) is hybrid utilitarian kitsch mellowed by old age: can-can girls display their bloomers on a ceiling mural, plastic crabs dangle above the frantic little marble-topped bar, tablecloths are checked, chairs are leatherette. White-jacketed waiters hurtle through the room carrying plates of oysters.

Some first courses are *à la mode* – like a smoked chicken and avocado salad; most stick to the traditionally briny route of shellfish or smoked fish. The menu is mostly sole, halibut or turbot: grilled, poached or fried. There are a few exotic intruders too: monkfish and dorade. Some elaborate preparations are in evidence and probably avoidable: the thing here is the best fish and shellfish, simply and accurately cooked. Helpings are huge and there aren't any mincing little garnishes cluttering things up. Vegetables are okay if hardly the kitchen's forte. Chips are the real thing. The sauce tartare could perhaps stand a bit of improvement – otherwise there's not much to fault. House white is goodish, cold and cheap; more sophisticated drinkers can zero in on the section of the wine list headed 'for the more discerning palate'. Pudding and coffee are serviceable. Over-indulgent or uncontrollably amorous diners can take advantage of the hotel upstairs: at £40 per double room it makes a quick afternoon game of how's-your-father just about affordable.

Mao Tai

58 New Kings Road,
London SW6
Tel: 01-731 2520
Mon-Fri 12 to 2.30, 7 to 11.45
Sat 7 to 11.45
Sun 12.30 to 3, 7 to 11.45
ACCESS, AMEX, DINERS, VISA
££

> Good for: *Sunday dinners, discreet lunching*
> Caveats: *Poor house wine*

Although the Golden Duck has been peddling upmarket
Chinese food in SW10 for yonks, it's only in the last five
years that Chinese food (that is the proper stuff not the Jade
Garden takeaway variety) has moved out of the Soho ghetto
and into the yuppie hinterlands. Norman Wong has been
one of the great missionaries spreading the word of crispy
duck to the affluent BMW-driving masses of Southwest
London. As manager of the Red Pepper in Park Walk he
cheerfully dispensed deftly cooked Pekingese and Szechuan food to the jeunesse hooray; he then moved west to
set up shop in P(arsons) Green. And the P Greenies flock
here: after a hard day's work at the estate agent's or the soft
furnishings shop Johnny and Amanda are absolutely dying
for a treat. As a result this place is often noisy and
drinks-partyish and impossible to get into on a spur of the
moment whim for 'some Chinese'. It is coolly hip (or should
that be coolie hip) in the post-trattoria modern style: there
are, of course, cesca chairs, and bare board floors and
ragged walls to indicate more than a nodding acquaintance
with *Interiors*. The waiters are smartly togged, too, with
white aprons, wing collars and red bow ties.

The cooking is pretty consistent – a major accomplishment in London Chinese restaurants – and can hit some high spots. The mostly Szechuan menu is littered with little red flames indicating 'hot and spicy', in other words lethal, dishes. The very unadventurous could construct a dinner reminiscent of the old days of Mister Chow – crispy fried 'seaweed', crispy duck etc – and be perfectly happy. The more progressive will be well rewarded too. Smoked chicken shreds in a light batter are a crisp and tangy first course: the salt and pepper squid can be utterly sensational, but has been known to be a little overtired too. Fish is good quality and usually well handled: the bass in hot bean sauce is luscious, the hot chilli prawns with bamboo shoots rather invigorating. The crispy aromatic duck with pancakes is no better or worse than in most upmarket Chinese trats. Beef and lamb are good quality and nicely cooked – the restaurant sometimes roars with the sound of sizzling lamb slices being rushed across the dining room on red-hot iron plates – and the chicken, particularly in spicier dishes, is good too. When they say 'garlicky' they aren't kidding. The 'home style' beancurd and vegetables and the Singapore fried vermicelli are better than average. Service is good, the atmosphere is rollicking but sophisticated. House wines are very so so: lager is a better bet.

Martinez

25 Swallow Street,
London W1
Tel: 01-734 5066
Mon-Fri 12.30 to 2.30, 6.30 to 12
Sat 6.30 to 12
Sun 12.30 to 2.30, 6.30 to 12
ACCESS, AMEX, DINERS, VISA
££

> Good for: *Tile fanciers, late-night Rioja*
> Caveats: *Tired cooking*

A friend says that this place is the best restaurant serving
the worst food in town. He's not too far off the mark.
Spanish food is indeed poorly represented in London, perhaps nowhere more so than here, but this restaurant still
has a lot of thrills to offer. It is a monument to 1920s Iberian
romanticism. Turn left through the front door and have a
pre-lunch or dinner drink in the sherry bar. Surrounded by
masses of post Inquisitional ironwork, faïence-topped
tables and a stuffed bull's head you'll feel like an extra in
The Return of Zorro. You climb up a hugely grand staircase
to the dining room, which must be one of the most
breath-taking restaurant interiors in London: the walls are
covered with spectacular majolica tiles depicting man's
inhumanity to beast in the guise of fowling, pigsticking and
so on.

The menu is long, chatty and churrigueresque. How
about some 'freshly poached chicken in Rioja wine with
almonds'? It 'must be tried once in a lifetime'. Or perhaps
Pato Sevillano – a 'succulent duckling cooked with affec-
tion'. For the incurably British, Thursday's dish of the day is
boiled silverside. It is best to begin simply – you can get a

decent tomato stuffed with crabmeat. More elaborate first courses can be bland and uninteresting. 'Once in a lifetime' chicken is perfectly all right; paella is merely a heap of mildly exoticised stodge. Some of the more basic fish dishes are okay; the vegetables a mere gesture. A large pudding trolley is laden with complex and sticky sweets. Service from proper grown-up waiters is a confusing mixture of resignation, irascibility and good humour. You can drink some nice Spanish wine here. A vacant bandstand promises late nights of wild zarzuelas.

AEROPORTO DI NAPOLI

apicella '87

Le Mazarin

30 Winchester Street,
London SW1
Tel: 01-828 3366
Mon-Sat 7 to 11.30
ACCESS, AMEX, DINERS
££

Good for: *Treats, photogenic sweeties*
Caveats: *Minuscule loos*

I didn't like this place very much when it opened up shop, but there's been a considerable jollification of surroundings and staff, and chef René Bajard – Roux brothers acolyte – is really cooking to win. This must now be one of the best restaurants with serious culinary intent in town and maybe the best value too. The catacomb-like dining rooms have been brightened with many licks of pink paint, an acreage of mirrors and an outburst of vinous Ronald Searle cartoons. Like a smart French restaurant in the provinces the linen is correct and the crockery is ugly. As soon as the plate of amuse-gueules – little bits of puffed pastry with halved not-quite-hard-boiled quails' eggs, warm tomato canapés – arrives you know that you're in for a treat.

The menu is short and seductive. You might begin with a glamorised peasant dish like superb warm lyonnais sausage with some tiny parsleyed potatoes or something altogether grander like a wobbly heap of warm and quite unbelievably light salmon mousseline. Anything with pastry – say the feuilleté of mussels – is excellent. Garnishes, such as a carved radish, can look heavy-handed. Main courses are cooked with a joyful verve and conviction. There is precision and delicacy here, but nothing the least bit namby-pamby. Pheasant is three huge breast slices lightly sautéed and served up with a confit of red cabbage and a potent sauce. A hefty grenadine of veal is perfectly cooked and arrives with splendid fresh noodles. Fish is beautifully cooked. Vegetables get perhaps a slightly too refined treatment – high-class baby food – but the little potato cakes are superb. The cheeseboard is first rate; puddings – délice aux deux chocolats – balance the voluptuous with a light touch. The plate of goodies served with coffee – little strawberry tartes, elephant ears, truffles – is too good to leave. Service from young black-tied French staff is efficient and downright cheerful. Clientele appears to be mostly earnest readers of food columns, foreigners and members of the gourmandising class of City Poo-Bah. The wine list is short and steepish: house wines are thankfully well chosen and easy on the wallet.

Le Métro

28 Basil Street,
London SW3
Tel: 01–589 6286
Mon–Fri 7.30 to 11, 12 to 2.30, 5.30 to 10.15
Sat 7.30 to 11, 12 to 2.30
Sun 8 to 11 am
AMEX
£

> Good for: *Fuel before Harrods, Saturday lunch*
> Caveats: *Overly intimate seating*

This cheerfully bustling little establishment lives in the cellar of No. 28 Basil Street, the small hotel owned by its bigger and grander neighbour the Capital (*q.v.*). The Métro is, I suppose, a wine bar, but far removed from the quiche-peddling brigade. The wine list is sensational and the food smart French which would do credit to many more elaborate (and expensive) places. There are, of course, bentwood chairs and a parquet floor and dragged walls. A huge cruover machine – a system which prevents open bottles of wine from spoiling and so allows the sale of single glasses of important stuff – dominates the rather cramped bar. Seating space, by the way, is hardly generous.

The short and attractive menu is augmented by daily specials displayed on one of those signboards you see in French cafés. The soup here is always excellent and warming and the mackerel in oil tastes of France, but the first course to go for is the superb warm chicken liver salad. Main courses veer towards the bourgeois. They do a correct and commendable blanquette de veau and a good lamb steak with Dijon mustard sauce. Fish and chicken are treated decently as well. Vegetables are of the gratin dauphinois, ratatouille variety. Cheeses are excellent and well kept – a further inducement to plunder the wine list. Coffee, served inevitably in those dark green gold-trimmed cups, is strong and excellent. Service by young waitresses is informal, dazzlingly hectic and inexplicably efficient. Lunchtime is noisy and crushed but the best time to observe the salesgirls from Harrods cosmetics hall out of their natural environment. The evening is rather quieter. It is more than just a handy watering hole in under-restauranted Knightsbridge: it should be an object lesson in running good, cheap and interesting restaurants. If only there were more like it. They serve breakfast too.

Mon Plaisir

21 Monmouth Street,
London WC2
Tel: 01-836 7243
Mon-Fri 12 to 2.15
Mon-Sat 6 to 11.15
NO CREDIT CARDS
££

> Good for: *Covent Garden, Jean Gabin Fans, fireplace in back room*
> Caveats: *Food, service*

Restaurant love is blind too. Mon Plaisir is probably one of the half dozen establishments that might be tagged as 'much loved' – still popular, but for reasons long gone. We can only assume that once upon a time the look and the feel and the service were unpretentious MOR Gallic; a whiff of the 'real' France. The look is still pretty satisfying – one of those inexplicable concatenations of bad taste that the French are so good at turning into a pleasing whole. So the printed brick wallpaper dado and the checked table-cloths and the 'Carte Gastronomique et Vinicole de France' are comforting and reassuring. As are the jocular notices: 'Moyenne de la vie humaine. 69 ans pour un buveur d'eau: 96 ans pour un buveur de vin. A vous de choisir.' (Surprisingly there isn't one of those lithographs of anthropomorphic dogs widdling.) Waiters in white shirts and black moustaches greet you with the spent hostility of legionnaires after a day's square bashing in the tropics. Their graceless arrogance ('Coca cola? No we don't have American champagne') almost makes you long for the phoney good humour of the local trat.

But the food is the real problem here: someone in the kitchen seems to think that bourgeois cooking is slapdash second-rate fodder. A plate of mixed hors d'oeuvre was poorly assembled and presented. The grated carrots were okay; the sardine was 'high', the potato salad strangled with mayonnaise. A first course off the blackboard was slightly better: cold mussel salad was tasty if a little too *fatigué* for comfort. Main courses ain't *vaut le voyage* either. An entre-côte was tasty but far too tough; chips were limp and mealy. Even a simple old standard like blanquette de veau was no good – fibrous veal in a tasteless watery sauce. Vegetables can be decent. The high point of lunch or dinner is purely extraneous – coffee sugar is presented in a fifties plastic globe dispenser emblazoned 'Ricard'. The location is a plus: the Covent Garden/Soho hinterlands aren't chockablock with restaurants and at least Mon Plaisir is too dowdy to attract Porsche-loads of media bimbos.

Montpeliano

13 Montpelier Street,
London SW7
Tel: 01-589 0032
Mon-Sat 12.30 to 3, 7 to 12
NO CREDIT CARDS
££

Good for: *After viewings at Bonham's*
Caveats: *Dispiriting for the ugly*

After San Lorenzo (*q.v.*) this is the most dead-glamorous Italian restaurant in Knightsbridge, peddling fettucine to a clientele which appears to be a hazy mix of Chanel jewellery, unseasonal suntans and an interest in racing cars. The chaotically multi-level dining rooms are chic if perhaps now looking – with their Lichtenstein prints – a teeny bit dated. Tennis fans should request the table beneath the portrait of Bjorn Borg or his framed Dornay tennis racket. There is a wild terrazzo floor and an over-abundance of hanging greenery. The grown-up table settings are more than a little marred by butter presented in airline-style foil-wrapped pats.

The menu is promising and more adventurous than some: you could have grilled radicchio for example. There are, of course, crudités for the ladies who lunch and more substantial first courses like an excellent porcini risotto. The bresaola is, as you'd expect, well bought; mozzarella in carozza (best described as a fried cheese sandwich) is delicious but maybe just a bit too substantial. As in so many Italian restaurants the simpler main courses are the best. So if you really want to eat well here choose one of the more interesting first courses and then move on to something like a grilled baby chicken which, though not exactly earth-shattering, will be perfectly well cooked. Fish is decently treated and the crab is good too. One thing worried me: my green salad was followed shortly by a waiter bearing a little dish of creamy glop. 'What's that?' I asked. 'Special Italian dressing,' the waiter answered. I have never in any decent restaurant in Italy ever had a salad dressed with anything other than oil and vinegar (or lemon juice). Why do they need special Italian dressing here – is it mindless invention or cynicism about the British taste'? That quibble aside, this is a jolly place with enough bustle to be stimulating and with decent cooking and rather energetically friendly service. You might want to forego pudding here and amble twenty yards down the road to Gran Gelato where the best Italian ice cream in London is dispensed in a Dinah Casson designed post-modernist setting.

Le Muscadet

25 Paddington Street,
London W1
Tel: 01-935 2883
Mon–Fri 12.30 to 3, 7.30 to 11
Sat 7.30 to 11
ACCESS, VISA
££

Good for: *Cheese, after Madame Tussaud's*
Caveats: *Offhand cooking*

With commendable lack of pretension Le Muscadet almost flaunts its Marylebone shopfront location: the big plate glass windows well display the passing life of Paddington Street. Inside, the look and feel of the place is no-nonsense bourgeois. The 'rustic' chairs are rush seated, the walls are white brick with a dark wood dado: there's a discreetly patterned brown carpet which runs up the front of the bar and odd arrangements of dried flowers. Genteel if rather bloodthirsty pictures – taken from Orme's oriental field-sports, I think – are closely hung: you may sit beneath 'Chase After a Wolf' or 'The Dead Hog'. A blackboard scrawled with the day's specials and the special wines of the month augments the printed carte.

The food here occasionally forays in the direction of modernism only to retreat back into familiarity. There may be some odd lapses of presentation. Take the mach salade for example: an unoriginal but a more than tasty concoction of bacon, croûtons and lamb's lettuce served with the lettuce left in great clumps and in a shallow bowl combining to make neat or easy eating impossible. 'It's delicious, but I'm giving up,' a friend said. I fear there are a few too many concessions to mainstream English taste as well.

Tomate maison – tomato stuffed with prawns and celery – sounded promising. As delivered, the prawns and celery were swamped in what tasted like steak-house-issue cocktail sauce, perhaps England's least valuable gift to civilisation. Main courses are hearty and often countrified. Coq au Fleurie arrived in a white oval dish coated with a heavy brown sauce sporting a few button mushrooms: perfectly all right, but unlikely to set any gastronomic houses on fire. Estouffade of beef – another house speciality – was another workmanlike production. Vegetables – boiled potatoes (rather underdone) and french beans (rather over) – seemed to have received little consideration. Not all kitchens are, or need to be, inspired, but a little more spark here would be most welcome. The cheeseboard – supplied by Philippe Olivier – is vast and excellent and probably the high point of any lunch or dinner here. Coffee is decent enough: service veers unpredictably from *charmant* to *un peu* offhand. It is all reminiscent of an average restaurant in a French provincial backwater: they don't seem to have realised yet that even *les anglais* can't live on atmosphere alone. It is popular with local businessmen.

Nam Long

40 Frith Street,
London W1
Tel: 01-439 1835
Mon-Sat 12 to 3, 6 to 11.15
ACCESS, VISA
£

> Good for: *Unblocking sinuses, squid*
> Caveats: *Not for the unadventurous*

'Vietnam food is justly famous,' says the menu, 'for its unique flavour and becoming fashionable.' More fashionable in America perhaps but making inroads here: this is one of two Vietnamese restaurants in Frith Street. Even though it bills itself as 'Vietnamese and Chinese Cuisine' – and you can eat crispy duck, sesame prawn toast et al. – the Vietnamese cooking is the thing to go for. I like Vietnamese food for its sharp clear flavours and light touch. This place is small and really quite chic. The nappery is pink and proper, the woodwork neat and grey, the chairs pale bentwood. One wall boasts an astonishing and rather horrible hologram of a pouring champagne bottle.

Vietnamese imperial spring rolls, sensitively cooked and wrapped in lettuce, are the *de rigueur* first course or you may have prawn-paste-coated sugar cane. Soups are splendid, particularly the brick red – and red hot – hot and sour fish soup. Small pieces of grilled spicy beef come accompanied by, and to be wrapped up in, the thinnest, most translucent rice pancakes you've ever seen. The various seafood dishes are well cooked and don't pussyfoot with the chillies either. Deep-fried crispy squid is chewy, spicy and nicely filled with a stuffing of savour and some complexity. Crispy frogs' legs perhaps recall the days when

Saigon was the Paris of the East. Vegetables and noodles are good; puddings – lychees, banana fritters – rather ho-hum. Service is helpful and obliging behind a mask of deceptive cheerlessness. The clientele is surprisingly *bon ton*. There is a short wine list, beer is perhaps wiser.

The Neal Street Restaurant

26 Neal Street,
London WC2
Tel: 01–836 8368
Mon–Fri 12.30 to 2.30, 7.30 to 11
ACCESS, AMEX, DINERS, VISA
£££

Good for: *Wild mushrooms, rich publicists*
Caveats: *Treacherous menu*

The Neal Street is the restaurant of good taste *par excellence*, seemingly frozen in the brave new world of the early seventies when 'businessmen' discovered 'art'. Like the Hockney paintings on the walls this place is increasingly more of a period piece and less of a shocker. It is still very beautiful to look at, if ever so slightly bloodless. Hockneys and Stellas hang on the white brick walls, a ceiling fan whirrs, the flowers are always fresh and the cane-seated chairs elegantly support the broadening bottoms of the loyal and besuited clientele. In many ways it was the precursor of the hip eclectic restaurant now so beloved by young British chefs: the menu romps across Europe and increasingly reflects the Italo–Austrian–German–British c.v. of manager Antonio Carluccio. So Uncle Hans from Düsseldorf can chomp Bismarck herring whilst Aunt Carla from Brindisi toys with her crespolini.

117

The food here is astonishingly variable, perhaps more so than in any other high-priced (a green salad is £3) restaurant in town. The first courses are always a good bet: the crab parcels (crab wrapped in a pancake and served on a little pool of spinach sauce) are still delightful, as are the scrambled eggs with smoked eel, the gravadlax and the seasonal antipasti. Main courses are more problematical and often approach the dullness of hotel dining room food. Simplicity generally pays off: the fish is excellent and the steak and kidney pie just the ticket when your tummy needs traditional cosseting. Vegetables are some of the best in town and are served up in huge helpings with a variety and quality that shows that this kitchen certainly doesn't stint when it comes to buying. Service is correct though maybe overly labour intensive – there always appears to be an absolute furore of trolley traffic. Fungus lovers rejoice when autumn comes and there is an astonishing (in variety, quality and price) assortment of wild mushrooms and truffles to choose from. This restaurant is full of good intentions and has introduced and promoted many of the goods we now take for granted on fashionable menus, and if you choose carefully you can certainly eat well here. The big question is why are there so many culinary booby traps, particularly when the men involved (Carluccio, Sir Terence Conran and Oliver Gregory) are such arbiters of cooking and style? And particularly when the prices involved so often turn out to be heart-stopping.

Odins

27 Devonshire Street,
London W1
Tel: 01–935 7296
Mon–Fri 12.30 to 2.30, 7 to 11.30
Sat 7 to 11.30
AMEX
£££

> Good for: *Romance, bohemian luxury*
> Caveats: *Dress up*

This must be London's most romantic restaurant. The lighting is flattering, the atmosphere is quiet, but not hushed (sweet nothings won't be overheard by the neighbours); the service has just enough *longueurs* for extended games of intercoursal footsie-footsie. The style of this place is rich and expansive. The walls are closely hung with a dazzling collection of paintings that would do credit to any connoisseur's drawing room. The faded velour chairs are comfortable, the tables are big and the ceiling is high (even if it is incongruously covered in cork tiles).

As soon as you hit the table so does a plate of hot cheesy canapés neatly served by a formally dressed (black jacket, long white apron) waiter. Then the big menu with Hockney drawing – which, along with the wonderful pictures and generous approach, is another Peter Langan hallmark – arrives. Choice is sensibly limited. After you order, a basket of the biggest bread rolls ever (at least Big Mac size) arrives. First courses are almost dauntingly large. You might have a huge bowl of some heartening domestic soup like leek and potato or a rich gratin of mixed fish. There are some grander things, too, like a silky galantine of chicken studded with pistachio nuts and served with marinated vegetables or a really excellent terrine of sweetbreads. Presentation is no nonsense – good looking, but undecorated food served up on biggish white plates. Main courses are bold and unfanciful. Sometimes there's a slight twist: excellent pheasant is served with mustard sauce, for example, or a manly veal chop is garnished with pine nuts. Beef and fish are very good. Vegetables – like ratatouille, puréed carrots or broccoli – are properly cooked and served up on little

crescent-shaped dishes. The pommes dauphinoise are terrific. Puddings incline towards the fatty's favourites – such as rum and raisin cheesecake or chocolate truffle slice. Coffee is excellent; the wine list pricey, but redeemed by good cheapish house wines. Standards here have remained high over the years. The service is excellent, the cooking is pretty darned good and the atmosphere cosily sophisticated: lunch or dinner here is still a tip-top treat.

L'Olivier

116 Finborough Road,
London SW10
Tel: 01-370 4183
Mon 7.30 to 11.30
Tues to Sat 12.30 to 2.30, 7.30 to 11.30
ACCESS, AMEX, DINERS, VISA
££

Good for: *Proper French roasts*
Caveats: *Frightful service*

This spectacularly inconsistent restaurant, veering from
excellence to contemptuous mediocrity, is part of Pierre
Martin's celebrated 'chain' of restaurants which includes
Lou Pescadou and Le Quai St Pierre (both *q.v.*). You ring the
doorbell of a dingy shopfront and your reservations are
checked and coats taken in a minute reception area. Then
it's downstairs to the surprisingly airy dining room, decorated with bright bits of Provençal pottery and amateurish
flower paintings. There are French cane café chairs, pale
blue nappery and a discreetly patterned carpet. Waiters –
dressed like beached matelots in blue t-shirts and red
trews – bustle about.

The menu is aimed at meat eaters but nonetheless
accommodates most tastes. There are excellently composed salads, fresh pastas, a variety of fish and shellfish
and a number of rustic roasts. You might begin with an
excellent feuilleté of asparagus or a foie gras salad. The
pasta with fruits de mer is reliably good, but with wild
mushrooms it can be as gritty as the verge of the M25. My
own favourite first course is the mixed hors d'oeuvre, a
huge and pukka selection of things like lentil salad, grated
carrots and other Froggy vegetarian treats. The major

roasts, like saddle of lamb or chicken, are wonderfully well cooked. Fish dishes are often sloppily over-sauced. Vegetables – usually of the French beans/carrot purée school – are an afterthought. There is a good cheeseboard. The wine list is selective and expensive, with Muscadet going for a preposterous £9.50 a bottle. Service from the grudgingly bilingual staff is erratic, impatient and slightly unpleasant. This place which began so promisingly needs some management attention pronto.

192

192 Kensington Park Road,
London W11
Tel: 01-229 0482
Mon-Sat 12.30 to 3, 7.30 to 12
Sun 1 to 3
ACCESS, AMEX, VISA
£

> Good for: *Picky eaters, Sunday lunch, peddling unpublished novels*
> Caveats: *Too street cred for Aunt Ethel*

This is the prime watering hole for the Notting Hill tribe of youngish publishers, designers, telly folk and social lubricators. It probably has more regulars than any other London restaurant and sometimes seems more like a drinks party than a public establishment. Tchaik Chassay's conversion of this cramped and awkward space into one of the first notable post-modern interiors in London has worn well and has been softened into something approaching cosiness by the smoke of endless Marlboros and the spillage of much wine. This is where Alistair Little (*q.v.*) first reached star status, and the cooking of his successor, Angela Dwyer, hasn't let the side down. The menu remains short, sharp, seasonal and surprisingly cheap. Lunch is eaten upstairs in the bar and dinner downstairs in a dingily lit but comfortable room furnished with stained wooden tables and black leatherette PEL chairs. The minuscule kitchen decants straight into the dining room.

First courses are trendy-modernistic – like raw sea bream with soy and horseradish or marinated goat's cheese with black olives – and less contrived than they sound. Soup, served in big white bowls, is homely; smart-sounding concoctions like warm liver mousse are of at least as good a standard as you will find in a lot of supposedly grander restaurants. Main course cookery doesn't mess around either. Lamb in a red wine sauce is perfectly pink, confidently flavoured and served in abundance; steamed chicken in chive sauce is well cooked and good looking; fashionable fishes like red mullet are beautifully handled. Vegetables are given a proper unfussy treatment and side salads may contain goodies like cold French beans. There are tarty moussey puddings of quality. A large number of customers appear to wear smoked glasses, big jackets and hair gels: some even carry portfolios and talk about projects. Service from hip chicks is casually proficient. As this is a wine bar there are no spirits but there is accommodation for all sizes of appetites. The wine list is splendid but, alas, the prose of yesteryear – which once described a wine as 'decent, but dull' – is gone. Flashes of wit linger on the menu though: saddle of hare carries the footnote 'Watership Down. You've read the book, you've seen the film, now eat the characters.'

Orso

27 Wellington Street,
London WC2
Tel: 01-240 5269
Mon-Sun 12 to 12
NO CREDIT CARDS
££

> Good for: *Progressive Italian cookery, after theatre*
> Caveats: *Imperious kitchen*

This is probably the most ambitious Italian restaurant in London: sadly its kitchen is, more often than not, long on imagination and short on execution. It also has occasional flashes of the same surliness and cynicism that afflicts its sister restaurant Joe Allen's (*q.v.*). Like Joe's it's a basement joint, but altogether smarter. You walk down a flight of terrazzo steps with the jazziest concealed lighting of any Italian restaurant and into the large and light dining room. The peachy plaster walls are hung with black and white snaps of Italian and show business notables, the white nappery on the tables looks stiff and sparkling, the combination salt and pepper holders cum toothpick dispensers are neatly evocative of Italy.

The menu, rather pretentiously in Italian on one side and English on the other – looks hip and authentic. No chicken breasts with asparagus tips here. So you might face first courses like arugala and potato soup or wild boar ham. The tomato and mozzarella uses real buffalo mozzarella – yes, it really comes from water buffalo milk – plenty of fresh basil and decent olive oil. Fontina croquettes with ham and sage were crisply fried if overpowered by the sage. There's a handful of good innovative pizzas, too, like pizza with gorgonzola and Parma ham. Pasta, like spinach and ricotta,

125

ravioli or tagliarini with calamari and mussels, is only so so. Main courses can fail to deliver: delicious-sounding grilled stuffed swordfish was dry and perhaps didn't use the freshest swordfish you've ever tasted. Grilled chicken with olives was ultra bland. The waitress warned that broccoli and spinach with oil and lemon were going to be served at room temperature – they arrived freezing and flavourless. Everything is dished up on nice Italian pottery plates though. Puddings are *à la mode* and luxurious: tiramisu and ricotta cheesecake. The espresso could be better. Getting served by the waitresses in smart white shirts and long white aprons may take some time. The kitchen could learn a little humility. There is usually a sprinkling of famous theatre faces, a handful of well-known writers and a few ferocious lady executives.

La Pappardelle

253 Old Brompton Road,
London SW5
Tel: 01-373 7777
Mon-Sun 12 to 3, 6 to 12
AMEX
£

Good for: *Pizzas, after cinema*
Caveats: *Boring veg*

In the beginning was La Bersagliera, the Kings Road pizzeria beloved by Chelsea youth with back-combed hair,
loud voices and Oxfam trendy clothes. And it sent forth its
legions of camerieri and pizzaioli, one of whom opened the
Pasta Connection (25 Elystan Street, SW3) and two of whom
started La Pappardelle. Like its parent restaurant this place
is cheap and jolly and popular with visiting Italians, but
unlike the Bersag it is thankfully less crowded and mercifully less noisy. The shallow vaulted room is done up in a
mix of Neapolitan ferocity and laid-back Californianism:
the chairs, woodwork, salt and pepper shakers and even
the burglar alarm are fire-engine red and there are framed
prints showing an idyllic world of bikini-wearing beach
bunnies and seductive lilos. The gleaming granite-topped
tables are as spruce and shiny as the massive espresso
machine.

The pizzaiolo here must be one of the most talented
doughboys in the Western World – indeed their basic pizza
bread with a very light garlic and tomato sauce is one of the
best things you can eat in any restaurant in town. Like a lot
of Italian restaurants they serve some downright silly
things which either smack of cliché (chicken with, horrors,
mozzarella and tomato) or unnecessary elaboration, but

their straightforward honest cookery is pretty darned good. You will get very good pasta e fagioli (ideal for cold nights or hungover lunchtimes) and minestrone, and the canonical first courses like tuna and bean salad or mozzarella and tomato don't beat around the bush. Neither do the sauces – their broccoli and chilli could wake the dead. The pasta itself is spot on, the gnocchi fabulous. Main courses run the standard chicken breast-liver-steak-trout gamut. The liver is terrific, but they could use a slightly less liberal hand with the butter. Vegetables of the sauté potato-peas-spinach school are rather perfunctory. Coffee is excellent and the service by a troop of jean-clad young Italians has the right mixture of brio and professionalism. There is a short and serviceable wine list. It is all very good humoured and run with pride: in the sometimes rather cynical restaurant world it is gratifying to see somewhere do what it sets out to do so well and with so little fuss. On hot days the front doors are flung open and tables are decanted onto the pavement for a close look at the louche streetlife of greater Earls Court.

Lou Pescadou

241 Old Brompton Road,
London SW5
Tel: 01-370 1057
Mon–Sun 12 to 3, 7 to 2
ACCESS, AMEX, DINERS, VISA
££

> Good for: *Midnight feasts, moules*
> Caveats: *No booking*

The name is the Niçoise for 'fisherman', but even if you
didn't know that (and who does?) the painted slogans 'bar
de la marine' and 'café des pêcheurs' should alert you to
expect briny goings-on. It is the cheapest and most informal of Pierre Martin's clutch of restaurants (viz. La Croisette, Le Suquet, Le Quai St Pierre, L'Olivier) and like the
rest of them neatly evokes idyllic eating in the SOF. The
tablemats are Provençal fabric, the walls are rough cast
plaster, the floors are terracotta. Maritime kitsch abounds:
running lights, steering wheels, dolphin-shaped lamps,
lumps of coral, ship models, piscatorial plates and frightfully butch pictures of foredeck gorillas manhandling
twelve metres through force ten gales. Waiters are dressed
à la matelot: blue trousers and blue and white striped
t-shirts.

The menu looks compact, but turns out to be wonderfully
comprehensive, ranging from simple, fastish food (half a
dozen oysters or maybe a pizza) through to more complex
plats du jour. Stunning fish soup or soupe au pistou
(flavoured with garlic and basil) arrives in huge tureens. So
does the extraordinary pasta which you can have with basil
or fruits de. mer or palourde (vongole) sauce. The salade
niçoise served from a large glass bowl is (*pace* Jacques

Médecin who in his book *Cuisine Niçoise* insists that *la vraie salade niçoise* should not have cold cooked vegetables in it) absolutely correct: oak leaf lettuce, tuna, anchovies, crisp french beans, faultless little boiled potatoes and irreproachable vinaigrette. Main courses include a good range of fish – fresh and well cooked – and steaks. Fried squid is exceedingly tasty: crispily cooked to the exact degree of readiness in the lightest of batters. The pizzas are first rate; the pissaladière is dreamy perfection – a circle of deliciously crisp dough topped with gently stewed onions, anchovies and tiny black olives. Moules farcies are succulent and garlicky, moules marinières plump and juicy. The best pudding is a stunning apple tarte. Coffee is proper: black and invigorating. There is a short wine list or you can have house wine (served in 25 cl pitchers) or cider. Service careers crazily from brusque to engaging. In a previous life this restaurant was the site of Toddy's, an all-night Afro-Caribbean affair where late-night party goers would eat volatile kedgeree and drink 'non alcoholic' bucks fizz into the dawn.

Phoenicia

11-13 Abingdon Road,
London W8
Tel: 01-937 0120
Mon-Sun 12 to 12
ACCESS, AMEX, DINERS, VISA
£

Good for: *Vegetarians, alternative Sunday lunch*
Caveats: *Long on garlic*

Every meal in a Lebanese restaurant seems to begin with
the mystical manifestation of the Giant Tomato. The Giant
Tomato – always first prizeworthy at any village fête –
arrives in a metal basket surrounded by radishes, celery
and cucumber, all rather nice to munch on as you flick
through the lengthy menu, which is pretty evenly divided
between first courses (mezze) and main courses (mostly
grills with the odd stew). Mezze are the thing to go for. 'A
meal is a social occasion,' the menu advises. 'We have
always enjoyed sharing it. We expect you to try it our way.'
It is less authoritarian than it sounds. 'Our way' turns out to
be sharing a huge number of hot and cold hors d'oeuvre
which the indolent can order off a set menu. The more
adventurous will plough through the whole list on succes-
sive visits. You may wish to avoid the raw lamb's liver.
Otherwise excursions into fodder incognita will be well
rewarded. The hoummus and stuffed vine leaves are pretty
familiar stuff. Labneh (home-made cream cheese with a
trickle of olive oil), kibbeh nayeh (best described as steak
tartare made with lamb), lahm baajine (a sort of Lebanese
pizza topped with minced lamb), and grilled halloume
cheese are absolutely wonderful. The falafel – a dish incidentally claimed as a national speciality by both Egypt and

131

Israel – is a revelation: a perfectly fried mishmash of chickpeas and garlic with a dreamy sesame sauce. You eat all this stuff communally, straight from the plates it arrives on while pittas whizz across the tables. The very greedy or very conventional can proceed to a main course: they certainly know how to grill a mean kebab here. Puddings involve prodigious amounts of sugar, crushed nuts and flaky pastry. The Turkish coffee is almost impenetrable in thickness and caffein. Lebanese wine is good and expensive: the house white (French) usually does the trick. A recent redecoration was in danger of making the dining room a tick too modish, but there are enough Levantine knick knacks (marquetry tables, ornamental plates) to maintain the atmosphere. Fellow diners when not Lebanese have an irritating habit of looking like post-graduate sociologists. Service is charming and helpful, the loos are simply miles away. Should you drink too much post-prandial arrak (the fierce Lebanese spirit) you can wander into the shop next door and buy a miniature traction engine for £3,500.

Pizzeria Condotti

4 Mill Street
London W1
Tel:01-499 1308
Mon–Sat 11.30 am to midnight
ACCESS, AMEX, DINERS, VISA
£

> Good for: *Cheap Mayfair dating*
> Caveats: *No espresso*

Conceived as the world's hippest Italian restaurant, Apicella '81 faltered on high prices and uneven cooking: Enzo Apicella wisely changed it to this most superior Mayfair pizzeria. The long rectangular room almost outdoes the Saatchi collection in terms of what art dealers call 'wallpower'. You may sit opposite an arresting Joe Tilson labyrinth, an endlessly fathomless wood sculpture by Eduardo Paolozzi, one of Andy Warhol's celebrated soup tins or an Apicella cartoon. The decor is classic smart trat brought into the eighties: there are, of course, cesca chairs, round tables and little vases of flowers perfectly spotlighted by low-voltage lamps hanging from overhead tracks. A wax effigy of Apicella in chef's whites surveys the white tiled floors. The paper tablecloths are much used for sketching by the fashionable clientele of Voguettes, Tatlerites and 'communicators'.

The hand-lettered menu is *au courant* and neatly balanced between figure-loving salads and bulge-making pizzas. Tuna or crab salad is usually good, mozzarella is hit or miss. You could more trendily begin with crab and papaya salad. The pizzas are up to the excellent Pizza Express standard – thin, crisp and tasty dough generously topped with the endless variations of tuna/ancho-

133

vies/mushroom/mozzarella/capers and so on and so on. The limited selection of puddings is adequate and, more often than not, unnecessary. Inexplicably, there is no espresso, only rather mediocre filter coffee. Service is provided by a fleet of young Italians: white shirted and black bow tied. The wine list is inventive and cheapish. Lunchtimes are packed but you can munch thirst-making black olives in the window while you wait. Dinner is altogether calmer and more civilised. Crockery is cringe-making green Steelite – it gives the razor-thin smoked salmon an unearthly hue and really ought to go. The minute basement loos have wonderfully jolly tiles.

Pollyanna's

2 Battersea Rise,
London SW11
Tel: 01-228 0316
Mon–Sat 7 to 12
Sun 1 to 3
ACCESS, AMEX, DINERS, VISA
££

Good for: *Sunday lunch, Armagnac fans, transpontine civility*
Caveats: *Pseudish conversation, Noddy-land ethos*

What is so awful about gentrification is the way it so obviously transforms an otherwise blameless neighbourhood by the need to supply all the essential middle-class services on site. Out go ironmonger and house clearance man, in come wine bar, cheese shop, interior decorator, pram renovator. And the names! Within sight of this restaurant we have La Bouffe and Puddleducks and Just Williams. Barf me out as they say in California: twee can go too far. Whilst on matters onomastic, Pollyanna's ain't such a hot name either, conjuring up as it does a place where the waitresses wear dirndls and the customers eat curds and whey. But it is altogether a more serious restaurant than the name suggests. Sunday lunch, for example, veers just far enough off the traditional path to be interesting.

There is good cream of sweetcorn soup sadly marred by bits of diced red and green peppers or a dull but unembarrassing smoked chicken salad to begin with. Roast beef is rare and exceedingly good. The roast lamb gets top marks too in spite of a forbiddingly glossy sauce. Vegetables (cabbage, carrots and cauliflower) are well cooked with just a touch of misguided inventiveness (walnuts in the cauliflower?). Puddings are of the modern dinner-party type ('We've just bought one of those marvellous Italian ice-cream machines at Divertimenti'): good melon sorbet or excellent hazelnut ice cream in a pool of complexion-destroying chocolate sauce. The surroundings are pretty pleasant – bare board floors, trendy mid-seventies pink and grey walls, nappery and tablemats. The Sunday clientele is mostly local and consists of members of the new bourgeoisie: couples who wear track suits (so convenient for hopping in and out of the Porsche) and are involved in something vaguely 'creative'. There is a good and inventive wine list and a long list of Armagnacs. Weekday cooking appears to be more cosmopolitan and ambitious.

La Poule au Pot

231 Ebury Street,
London SW1
Tel: 01-730 7763
Mon-Fri 12.30 to 2.30
Mon-Sat 7 to 11.15
ACCESS, AMEX, DINERS, VISA
££

> Good for: *Old-fashioned romance, gastronomic cuddles*
> Caveats: *Overflowing vin, monolingual service*

When you order house wine they put a magnum on the table. Laws of human behaviour say that those who only want 'a glass of wine' will drink only a glass of wine no matter how much is on offer, but those who want more than a single glass will hoover up the lot. So, the line most overheard here is 'We might as well finish the bottle . . .' More than old-fashioned bistro Gallicism and bourgeois cooking have made this restaurant flourish unchanged. It is rather like the place where two characters in a situation comedy go for a date. Ze waiters are verrey verrey Frennch and zey speak ze English onnly wiz ze grate raylooktance. Ze decor she is verrey verrey French too: the walls are bare brick; the woodwork is the colour of mousse au chocolat; a cartwheel hangs above the fireplace; the dangling light fixtures are baskets of artificial fruit. The crockery is cobbled together provincial – a jumble of blue willow, hearty coaching scenes and neo-delft.

The menu is written on a blackboard. You might begin with a quiche or a cream soup: the soup is thick and honest, the quiche rich and buttery with decent pastry. Or you might want to be adventurous and try something like the salad of shredded gruyère, raw spinach and croûtons in a garlicky dressing – a weird but not unpleasant French interpretation of a Caesar salad. Main courses are pretty good – the most predictable are the best. The poule au pot is good on hostile winter nights – a hugely generous plate of boiled chicken and carrots, leeks and potatoes. The gigot is good too as is the blanquette de veau. Fish is not their strong point. Indeed all the cooking here relies on heartiness rather than finesse. Vegetables are slightly over-cooked and slightly over-buttered, but there are lots of them and they are served in help-yourself style. Cheese is simple – a huge slice of brie – and not particularly good. The bread is shockingly bad. It is a jolly, unfussy restaurant full of besuited businessmen by day and soon-to-be-snogging couples by night.

La Preferita

163 Lavender Hill
London SW1
Tel: 01-223 1046
Mon-Sat 12.30 to 3, 7 to 11.30
ACCESS, AMEX, DINERS, VISA
£

> Good for: *Confidential lunches, jolly pasta*
> Caveats: *Diabolical vinaigrette*

Of the scant handful of decent Italian resaurants south of the river, this one is the most favoured by residents of Clappers, Wanders and the other transpontine Sloane hinterlands. It is a capable and well-intentioned restaurant which could hold its modest own in any part of London. The ground-floor dining room is decorated with slickness and sensitivity – white tiles, a wide dark wood chair rail and a neatly hung and quite sparkling collection of Italian landscapes portraits and capricci. The atmosphere is lively, like a trattoria in a television series. Upstairs – reached by a narrow Himalayan staircase – is altogether more grave: a lino floor, a Peterjonesian Georgian chandelier and a roaring gas flame fire. Throughout there is pink nappery, bentwood chairs and big wine glasses.

The menu is standard issue: insalate tricolore, seafood salad, minestrone and some of those funny main courses with molten mozzarella. What there is can be very good, but there are sometimes inexplicable lapses. So a huge, neatly cooked and trimmed artichoke was nuked by an utterly disgusting creamy (yucch) vinaigrette. (Salad eaters N.B. or you'll get the same too. Olive oil is there for the asking.) Spaghetti cennarino with tomato, chillies and basil was properly cooked if a little timid on the basil front. They offer more fish than most modest trats and serve it well: a frito misto was crisp and fresh, not the usual dustbinful of over-tired whitebait and frozen scampi that so many places peddle. Calves' liver with sage is good, too, as are the steaks. Vegetables are run of the mill and so is the trolleyload of puddings. Coffee is okay and the wine list is concise and well selected. House white is good and cheap. The service from a staff of white-shirted and long-aproned waiters is superb: friendly and enthusiastic without the I'm-greeting-you-like-my-long-lost-cousin-Angelo-from-Calabria hoo ha.

Le Quai St Pierre

7 Stratford Road,
London W8
Tel: 01-937 6388
Mon 7 to 11.30
Tues–Sat 12 to 2.30, 7 to 11.30
ACCESS, AMEX, DINERS
££

> Good for: *Oysters, Porsche drivers*
> Caveats: *Distracted sauces*

For over ten years Pierre Martin has been a hero of the London restaurant world. His first restaurant here, La Croisette, was an absolute revelation: someone actually succeeded in opening a fish restaurant in London that would do credit to many a French town. His success was immediate and deserved. La Croisette begat Quai St Pierre, Le Suquet, L'Olivier and Lou Pescadou: certainly the best 'chain' of restaurants in London and all worthy of a place in anyone's list of the best. There isn't much really to choose between La Croisette, Le Suquet and this place, only the most minor gradations of food and mood, because they all serve up the same miraculously fresh fish and shellfish in a credibly Provençal atmosphere. It is indeed just a little bit amazing that a few quayside gouaches, some Brother Sun tablemats and the promise of half a dozen decent oysters can easily dispel the gloom of London's worst weather. I can't say Le Quai St Pierre is the best of Martin's places but it is certainly the smallest, although its attractively titchy charms pale at some of the exceedingly cramped upstairs tables.

The shellfish here is en masse the best in London: even though I'm a fan of the oysters at Wilton's, Green's and

Sweetings I ultimately prefer the French fines claires here. And if you like rubbery briny things like winkles you'll be well served, too, particularly if you order the plateau de fruits de mer – a large cork board bearing an encyclopaedic assortment of crustacea. The moules are splendid as well. If you don't like wrestling with shells you might want to begin with something like a feuilleté of asparagus. After the splendours of the first courses what follows can be a little bit disappointing. Your sole or turbot or mullet will be worthy of Jacques Cousteau's scrapbook, but maybe they're just a little let down by the cooking. Sauces sometimes overwhelm and pastry cases sometimes fail to convince. Here, as in many other fishy establishments, simplest is best. Tarte tatin is the jolliest pudding. Waiters wait with grim, harassed efficiency. The clientele is well groomed and cashmerian. A tankful of contented lobsters play, oblivious to the sound of their brothers being happily gulped.

Read's

152 Old Brompton Road,
London SW5
Tel: 01-373 2445
Mon-Sun 12.30 to 2.30
Mon-Sat 7.30 to 11
ACCESS, AMEX, DINERS, VISA
££

> Good for: *Sexy lunches, puddings*
> Caveats: *Staff hauteur*

High-class jeweller Colin Crewe (brother of traveller, food writer and co-owner of Grill St Quentin, Quentin Crewe) set up this stylish and at first rather overwrought restaurant in conjunction with Keith Read and his cooking wife Caroline. Well, Caroline no longer cooks here, the restaurant has expanded and redecorated and the more fanciful aspects of the menu have been toned down or disappeared altogether. The visual style of the place would seem to owe a lot to mid-eighties Conran shop taste, a slick blend of the provincial and the ethnic – big cane chairs with bright cushions, bold Indian natural history paintings, a whirring ceiling fan. One of the new downstairs dining rooms has been smartly trompe-l'oeiled into a conservatory. Alas, the service is not always as comforting as the upholstery – some women have been bullied for not ordering wine so I hope in future they'll watch their staff more carefully. Lunches are uncrowded and something of a bargain; dinners rather more social and expensive.

Soups like carrot and watercress are always good; other first courses are less homely. A salad of guinea fowl and lamb's liver with warm hazelnut dressing was tasty and proficient. I like Sunday lunch here, when the main courses are just on the adventurous side of traditional cookery. Their very rare roast beef with rosemary is superb, as is the salmon, which shows that they can do the simple (but not necessarily easy) things with style and finesse. Even the unpiggy will have some difficulty resisting the puddings. The slightly unorthodox trifle is a megacalorific concoction of blueberries, bananas, strawberries and whipped cream and is a pleasant danger to health and morality. Coffee is good but the house wines are not up to scratch. It is much favoured by the cosmopolitan residents of the greater Boltons, the gold-card carrying and the grown-up. Their delicatessen next door sells wine, coffee beans and made-up main courses to raise the tone of bachelor dinner parties.

The Ritz

Piccadilly,
London W1
Mon–Sat 12.30 to 2.30, 6.30 to 11
Sun 12.30 to 2, 7.30 to 10.30
ACCESS, AMEX, DINERS, VISA
£££

Good for: *Treats, decorative paintwork*
Caveats: *Too many spivs*

The Ritz has always been beautiful; even when the hotel and restaurant weren't quite up to scratch, their many faults were forgotten in the Mewes and Davis powerful essay in neo-*ancien régime* decor. The dining room is the most splendid in London. Marble and gold ionic columns rise beneath a vertiginous oval of trompe-l'oeil sky, the walls are pink and green marble panels; gilt chandeliers of astonishing complexity circle the room, Green Park beckons through the windows and there are enough niches, swags and decorative doodahs to inspire a thousand wedding cakes. The cooking, alas, is not always so sublime. Much-hyped chef Michael Quinn arrived to revolutionise the staid kitchens but was unable to generate much excitement in the vast and conservative establishment – he now cooks at a country house hotel.

The new culinary regime carries on the balancing act of traditional versus modern. Even though you enter the restaurant past a buffet laden with immemorial plutocratic goodies – mammoth asparagus, split lobsters, feathered game – there is also altogether more adventurous food. So Parma ham and melon will be well selected, smartly presented and, of course, utterly predictable, but a salad of warm scallops, bacon and designer lettuce is nicely progressive and confidently assembled. Grills and roasts are as well prepared as they should be in a hotel of this standard: your rich godfather will be pleased with his lamb cutlets or roast partridge. More inventive dishes – like pan-fried brill with forest mushrooms – are good but don't have the snap or sparkle to lift them out of the slightly gloomy netherworld of 'hotel cookery'. Service is efficient and dignified. Fellow diners can disappoint – too many 'businessmen' in grey patent loafers, too many over-groomed American women. The wine list is comprehensive and dauntingly priced; the brandy snaps with coffee are free. The glamorous atmosphere is most palpable on the cabaret evenings when they have Cole Poteresque entertainment, mostly imported from New York.

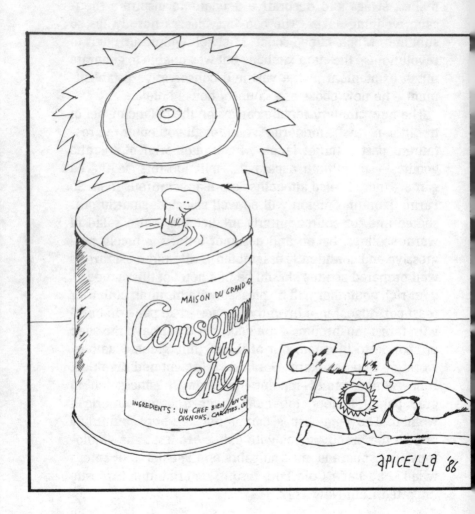

Rouxl Britannia

Trident Court,
Finsbury Square,
London EC2
Tel: 01-256 6997
Mon-Fri 12.30 to 2.30
ACCESS, AMEX, DINERS, VISA
£

> Good for: *Gastronomic relief near the Square Mile*
> Caveats: *Canteen like*

Sitting at the top of a vast and multi-million-pound gastronomic empire (they make pâtés for Marks and Spencers
and lunches for French office workers as well as catering
for international fat cats at Le Gavroche and the Waterside
Inn), Albert and Michel Roux are entrepreneurs as well as
celebrated chefs. Their latest field of endeavour is 'sous
vide' cookery – rather irreverently called boil-in-the-bag –
a method in which food is cooked in a vacuum and then
reheated before serving. Sous vide means that food can be
prepared to standard in a central kitchen-factory and then
sold at virtually chefless restaurants. The punter gets consistently high-class food at knock-down prices, the entrepreneur saves on chefs' salaries, rental of kitchen space
and bulk buying. The Roux brothers want to broadcast their
cooking through the sous vide medium and Rouxl Britannia
is the first in their projected chain. It perches in a corner of
Trident Court, a splendid example of neo-baroque archi-
tecture recently tarted up American fashion with an atrium
and dour security men sitting behind marble desks. The
restaurant itself is brightly if unimaginatively decorated
with white tiles, *belle époque* sconces, black granite-topped
tables and plastic rattan French café chairs. The walls are
hung with what I believe are called financial instruments:

you may, for example, sit beneath an Imperial Chinese Government Bond.

The menu – a nifty farrago of French and English favourites – is dazzlingly bilingual: you may wish to know that potted kippers are *pâté de harengs fumés* in frogspeak. They are jolly tasty, too, as is the potted tongue with horseradish sauce. A rather more *haute* first course – scallop mousse – was less successful. Main courses run the gamut from serviceable to very good. Grilled lamb is perfectly all right, roast wing of skate with parsley sauce is much better. Vegetables are unexciting. There is a plat du jour in addition to the printed menu. The francophone waitresses may offer you a little some-hair-poo-ding for dessert which is a bit too sweet, or maybe walnut ice cream which is better. At £12.50 the set menu (three courses) is a bargain and the house wines do the trick at a reasonable price. The downstairs café is considerably cheaper. On the northern fringe of the City, Finsbury Square is certainly *vaut le voyage* and unlike the City (where they close half an hour earlier) the banks here are open 'til 3.30: at least there is a tiny capitalist corner in the people's republic of Islington.

San Frediano

62 Fulham Road,
London SW3
Tel: 01-584 8375
Mon-Sat 12.30 to 2.30, 7.15 to 11.15
ACCESS, AMEX, DINERS, VISA
££

> Good for: *Saturday lunch, jolly vegetarians*
> Caveats: *Bring ear-plugs*

It is the jolliest, noisiest, Sloaneist trat and also probably the best. If the whole place were freeze dried a future anthropologist could reconstitute the social life of middle-class London circa the last third of the twentieth century. The decor is classic Apicella with a rustic touch: you sit on red rush-seated chairs. Unless you are very lucky you wait for your table in the minuscule bar: the fortunate perch on stools, the rest stand and drink their camparis and soda. The two long and narrow dining rooms are unbelievably cramped, but at least each table has a decent view of what must be the most appetising hors d'oeuvre trolley in London. Astonishingly energetic waiters weave their way through at high speed, rarely making mistakes and displaying amazingly good cheer to regulars and newcomers. There are a lot of couples who have been coming here for years, from dinner dates as bright young things when she shared a flat with three other girls in Onslow Square to treats as respectable marrieds when he drives an Audi and they own a house with a garden big enough for the kids in Clapham. There are occasionally flash intruders – the odd bimbo in stretch pants who after a boozy lunch drags her boyfriend across the road to spend some money on her at Butler & Wilson – but the general tenor of the place is well bred.

This is one of the few old-established restaurants that doesn't slip. There is a large but undaunting menu: printed on the left and handwritten on the right. The pasta is good whether it's just a simple spaghetti with tomato sauce or a more exotic and ravishing dish of black noodles. Other first courses, like the mushrooms and the stuffed tomatoes, are fresh and unmucked about. The main course standbys are well cooked and plainly presented: grilled chicken is tender and delicious, liver with sage isn't swimming with butter and the vitello tonnato is prepared to the book, but with spirit. Vegetables and salads (like radicchio dressed with oil) are good and interesting enough to amuse vegetarians. Puddings are proficient but dull – the only thing here that is absolutely average. The strong and good coffee is still being poured in enormous quantity from the famous and increasingly chipped red enamelled coffee pots. San Fred's is an exemplary high-volume restaurant – and I don't mean the shrieking of the customers: it has a huge turnover and obligingly passes the benefits on to us: high quality ingredients (nothing gets a chance to hang about) and lowish prices.

San Lorenzo

22 Beauchamp Place,
London SW3
Tel: 01–584 1074
Mon–Sat 12.30 to 3, 7.30 to 11.30
NO CREDIT CARDS
££

> Good for: *Lunchtime ogling, carpaccio*
> Caveats: *No credit cards*

In spite of major redecoration little has changed here, although the famous sycamore tree has died and been turned into bas-reliefs by Joe Tilson. The clientele is getting older and perhaps even richer. *Soignée* women – ex-Voguettes, former models, wives of shipping magnates or even all three – still lunch here in gaggles to talk about the day's shopping or the coming night's charity bash. There is a fair sprinkling of famous faces too. The men are as often as not foreign or at least tanned, and some of them still wear Gucci loafers with chinks. Late sixties chic is in the air here: there are tiled floors, white walls hung with Warhol prints of Marilyn Monroe, cane chairs and a profusion of green plants.

The menu is presented stapled onto a rattan tablemat. A colossal selection of crudités with bagna cauda – the delicious garlicky dip – is a favourite here (so good for slimming) as is the fiery penne all'arrabbiatta (excellent for hangovers). Unlike the food in a lot of London Italian restaurants what you eat here often tastes like the real thing. Produce is first rate too: so your prosciutto will not be elastic and the mozzarella (for an admittedly hefty surcharge) will be the stellar product made from water buffalo milk. Baked eggplant with mozzarella and tomato sauce is

149

gutsy, fresh and ungreasy. Risotto nero is another ballasty first course. They do game and pigeon (casseroled in a rich sauce with polenta) well. Fish is often presented simply, as in grilled mackerel with rosemary. The fritto misto is varied and generous if sometimes in need of a bit more concentration from the man who looks after the boiling oil. The liver is terrific; vegetables less so, often overcooked and overbuttered.

Ice cream is excellent; espresso potent. The wine list is interesting but unshy about demanding high prices like £7.50 for house white. The greeting may be slightly stern but service from the blue-aproned waiters is charming and proficient.

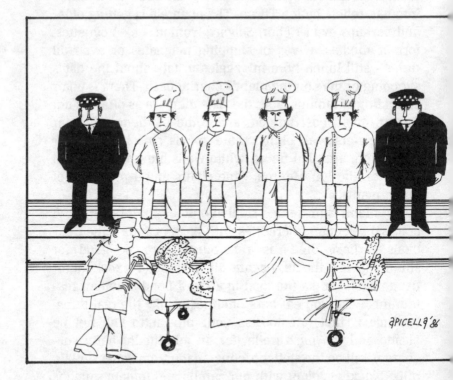

Santini

29 Ebury Street,
London SW1
Tel: 01-730 4094
Mon-Fri 12.30 to 2.30, 7 to 11.30
Sat-Sun 7 to 11.30
ACCESS, AMEX, DINERS, VISA
££

> Good for: *Adventurous Italian cooking, flash harrys*
> Caveats: *Over-inventive saucing, noisy neighbours*

What an infuriating farrago of good culinary intentions, post-modernism and pretentious profundo this restaurant is. Its fashionability is undeniable – along with the serviceable Signor Sassi in Knightsbridge Santini was one of the first Italian restaurants to break the Apicella design mould (white walls/tile floors/bentwood chairs) and indulge in something closer to the sensibilities of progressive rag traders, North Londoners and people who winter in Antigua. The dusty rose floor tiles, the grey lacquer furniture, the Flos wall sconces, the waiters' kit of smart sleeveless pullovers and pastel bow ties all ooze good taste and high prices. But first you have to get in, unfazed by the sour fella at the front desk who eyes you with distaste and dispatches you to an appalling table.

The menu is a revelation, miles from the usual banalities of the dreaded London Italian Restaurant, even if it does perhaps tend towards the over-complex (e.g. 'Agnello Regina: Lamb cutlets in a white wine and herb sauce with Regina grapes' – uuurgh!). Good things abound, though, and the menu ranges well beyond the Venetian food they curiously choose to specialise in. So you can get proper Italian grub here like fried courgette flowers or porcini risotto. Pasta can be outstanding: the pappardelle (broad flat noodles) with artichoke sauce are interesting, snappy and fresh tasting. There are some oddities though: what should have been straightforward penne all'arrabbiata (that is with tomato and chilli) was foolishly marred by extraneous red peppers. Standbys like grilled calves' liver, carpaccio and osso bucco are well cooked using sound ingredients. Vegetables are rather disappointing; a mingy little selection reminiscent of a jumped-up hotel dining room in the boondocks. The dessert trolley is huge and for once tempting, with lots of fresh fruit and a wicked chocolate torta. Coffee is good; the wine list full of promising vino. Customers incline towards the noisy, the boring ('He had five whiskies before lunch and then a brandy because he felt dry!'), and the overly *soigné* denizens of lower Belgravia.

The Savoy Grill

Savoy Hotel,
London WC2
Tel: 01-836 4343
Mon-Fri 12.30 to 2.30, 6 to 11.15
Sat 6 to 11.15
ACCESS, AMEX, DINERS, VISA
£££

> Good for: *Power lunching, roasts*
> Caveats: *Order carefully*

Largely thanks to the effort of kitchen wunderkind Keith
Stanley – who began here as one of the toy boy generation
of under-thirty-year-old chefs – this sometimes
just-a-bit-fusty restaurant has been changed into a rather
more exciting place to eat. Not that food is necessarily the
prime attraction here as this place is – along with Wilton's,
Les Ambassadeurs and a few other establishments – a real
theatre of tycoonery. If money talks this is the place to hear
it and the air is often thick with the likes of 'I know you
can't be too careful, Desmond, but we're not dealing with a
lot of little old ladies as investors' and similar expressions
of commercial probity. The look of the place is sleek and
somewhat anonymous: expensive wood panelling, brass
wall sconces and plush crescent-shaped banquettes comfortable enough for millionaires of any girth.

The menu neatly balances traditional grill-room fodder
with some of the more barking innovations of 'modern
British cooking'. If you go to a restaurant to eat things like
smoked salmon or beluga you can get them here and they
will be as good as if they came from a top-class delicatessen. If you want something that actually involves the kitchen, like a cold crab omelette with a light tomato sauce (I

know it sounds utterly diabolical) or a salad of scallops marinated in ginger, you won't be disappointed. Soups are good as well, though I could do without the fennel in the lobster bisque. There is a homely litany of plats du jour: bangers and mash (this being the Savoy, they call them 'Farmhouse sausages, creamed potatoes and fried onions'), roast beef, steak and kidney pie and roast duck. All are canonically cooked and served up with the proper trimmings. Succulent roasts arrive on huge silver trolleys and are dispensed with astonishing dexterity by a pukka white-uniformed carver. The right-hand side of the menu is the progressive half, providing the likes of loin of veal coated with duxelles and wrapped in lettuce in a bone marrow sauce. Sometimes innovation rapes common sense; sometimes dishes taste just a little tired (the curse of hotel food) and sometimes there is a blissful surprise like the chaudron de gibier, a most advanced game pie. The vast list of vegetables is well cooked. A heart-stoppingly expensive wine list is full of nobby bottles and is a minefield to the inexpert. Service is charming and cosseting. If you are spending your own money here rather than the shareholders' you might take advantage of the not-too-crippling pre-theatre menu.

Simply Nico

48a Rochester Row,
London SW1
Tel: 01-630 8061
Mon-Fri 12 to 2.30, 7 to 11.15
ACCESS, AMEX, DINERS, VISA
££

Good for: *Exciting cooking, ladies lunching*
Caveats: *Dour atmosphere*

Nico Ladenis is the problem child of British cookery. A
self-taught chef, he is appallingly scorned by the culinary
'establishment'. Arrogant and tactless, he is the scourge of
timid customers – being in his restaurant is like playing
with a loaded shotgun after too many Armagnacs. But (and
this is the biggest 'but' in restaurants) he is a chef of
tremendous verve, skill and daring who can sometimes
produce some of the best food you are likely to get in this
country. After a disastrous fling in suburban Reading, Nico
has set up in central London for the first time, albeit in the
slightly grim hinterlands of Victoria (although there is a
fine set of Victorian almshouses just down the road). This
new restaurant is small and quite clearly means business.
Decor is unobtrusive: pale greens and creams, *Directoire*
armchairs, Adamesque wall sconces and a mirrored chair
rail. The linen is dazzlingly white, the cutlery big and
simple.

Nico's cooking is more basic and intense than before:
this is one of those places where the flavours almost punch
you in the nose. The red mullet soup is one of history's
great fish soups: heady and powerful. Or you might want
another fishy first course like the amazing warm escalope
of smoked salmon. Salads are good: aggressively fresh,

155

served up on big plates, pretty but not over-arranged. Main courses are on the money too. There is wonderfully well-cooked lamb with a light garlic sauce or splendid tournedos of veal potent with rosemary. Vegetables are a revelation: cooked in sealed containers with clarified butter. When you eat a carrot here you actually want another. The pommes dauphinoise are dreamy, the galette of noodles a splendid surprise. There is a vegetable of the day – like baby mangetout – served family style as well. Cheeses are in top-flight condition and served with walnut bread or biscuits. The chocolate mousse with a light orange coulis is a treat for even the most jaded chocoholic. Service by waiters in black tie or waitresses in long black skirts is formal but friendly. The wine list ranges wide and tends to avoid clichés. In spite of the slightly grave demeanour of the place it's an exciting restaurant to be in because there is such a commitment here to dynamic, forceful and un-mucked-about cookery. The £16.50 set lunch (with no hidden extras) is a very good deal.

Singapura

839 Fulham Road,
London SW6
Tel: 01-736 9310
Mon-Sat 7.30 to 11
Sun by request
ACCESS, AMEX, DINERS, VISA
££

> Good for: *Orgasmic ice cream, volcanic chillies*
> Caveats: *Not for timid eaters*

This deft and dapper little restaurant in a railway carriage of a room shows among other things just how much the 'ethnic revolution' has changed London eating habits: ten years ago no self-respecting estate agent would be seen eating babi char rebong; now their BMWs are parked on the pavements outside. A dozen tables perch underneath lamps of ferocious modernism and amazing complexity, the white walls are hung with photographs of pre-war Singapore, the tiny mirrored bar sports a bookshelf full of repro Southeast Asian sculpture, the stereo hums with electric jazz. Table settings are basic and a small vase holds a sprig of Singapore orchids.

The longish menu is not too hard to get around: good descriptions and helpful staff can allay most fears of nervous eaters. You expect the satay (marinated skewered beef, chicken or pork with a pungent peanut butter sauce) to be excellent and it is, as are the fried marinated king prawns and the vegetable and prawn spring rolls. The seafood cookery here is adventurous: there is zippy and unusual plaice with tamarind and lemon grass and notable crab claws with chilli and ginger. When they say chilli they really mean it: the hot dishes here aren't for the weak of tongue. Chicken lam – a Cambodian dish of minced chicken and green chilli – is available on request to clear your sinuses and knock your socks off. Shark fishcakes – by advance order only – are exciting and fiery too. More mild-mannered tastes will be satisfied by the dishes cooked in coconut cream or the clay pot cookery. Vegetarians rejoice in the onion omelette, the aubergine with lemon grass and the bean curd with hot peanut sauce. I like the rice cooked in chicken stock with garlic and ginger and the vermicelli noodles with prawns. The Earl Grey, ginger or brown bread ice cream is probably the best in London. House wine is good value Sicilian but it may be wiser to stick to the cold and bracing Tiger lager from Singapore. For those bored with traditional roasts, they arrange jazz Sunday brunches with a set menu and a live trio pumping out the likes of Chattanooga choo choo.

Steamers

32 Putney High Street,
London SW15
Tel: 01-788 1900
Mon–Sat 12 to 2.45, 6 to 11.45
ACCESS, AMEX, DINERS, VISA
£

Good for: *Hip fish, after drinks parties*
Caveats: *Silly pasta*

A ramble along 'the slimy foreshore' (the phrase is John Gay's by way of Ben Weinreb) of Putney is a splendid appetite-raising exercise. In spring and summer the shambolic boathouses are pullulating with fours and eights; in the winter you can make out Fulham Palace through the bare trees across the river. Sad then that Putney is so ill equipped with decent restaurants. Indeed, if it weren't for this estimably intentioned establishment a chap could starve in SW15.

This place flogs Californiaesque cuisine, a pleasant farrago of health-junk and Mexican food rising to a fishy high point. California has been in the forefront of the 'rediscovery' of an often factitious American cuisine and here they at least touch bases with a few of the main strands. The dining room appears to be done up with the cast-offs from a production of *The Flying Dutchman*: you eat amidst a profusion of portholes, binnacles, gaffs and other maritime impedimenta. First courses hover in clichéville (prawn cocktail, deep fried potato skins, avocado vinaigrette) with a nod towards New England (clam chowder) and south of the border (guacamole): all pretty average really. You could then go on to the dubious pleasures of supreme of chicken St Louis or duck breast New Orleans (what, no turkey leg

159

Detroit?) but fish is the main point here. You can have quite superior shark, tuna, halibut or swordfish cooked either in the modish blackened style (coated with hot Louisian spices and nuked in a red hot skillet) or more simply grilled. Occasionally exotic intruders like maui maui turn

APICELL7 '86

up too. There's some passable, but rather contrived pasta: french fries and side salads are up to scratch. Coffee is described in Americanese as 'a bottomless cup – just ask for a refill'. Service is youthful and quite charming; the house wine okay; prices cheapish.

About Menus . . .

Restaurants are legally obliged to display a menu with prices inclusive of VAT. If the menu is displayed in an illuminated perspex box topped with French, German and Italian flags then turn tail and run. Ditto if it's headed 'Welcome, Willkommen, Bienvenue' – this isn't *Cabaret*.

In spite of often high cover charges and varying service charges the menu can give you a fairly reasonable idea of what it's going to cost you to get out once you've got in: just multiply the price of an average main course by three and you'll get an approximate price per head.

The menu should of course also give you a reasonable idea of what the food is like. Absurdly long or insanely global menus (lamb pasanda, tacos, chicken Kiev, boeuf stroganoff) mean trouble – lots of tinned, frozen or otherwise pre-prepared food. Watch out for clichés as well: calves' liver in raspberry vinegar could mean a chef resting on once fashionable laurels. Jocular headings – 'From Neptune's Net', 'Fresh from the Garden' and so on – hint at perilous dining within.

Standards of menu design and typography are generally frightful, but a menu that looks as if it is presented with care (even if in 'bad' taste) usually hints at effortful cookery.

Suntory

73 St James's Street,
London SW1
Tel: 01-409 0201
Mon-Sat 12 to 2.20, 7 to 10.20
ACCESS, AMEX, DINERS, VISA
£££

> Good for: *Keeping up with the future-sans, discretion*
> Caveats: *Unrelaxing*

My tape-recorder, compact disc player, stereo system, television set (yes, I do have a licence) and typewriter are all Japanese. Even the hubs and the gears on my bicycle are Japanese. But I, and I suspect we, will never ever understand the Japanese. The Restaurant Suntory (European flagship of the huge Suntory brewing and distilling empire) sits on St James's exuding dignity, sobriety and mega-yennery. As you pass through the reception area you are ushered into a small, tasteful and rather uncomfortable bar. And what are the first decorative objects of note in this rich, refined, sober atmosphere? A set of whisky bottles in the form of jocular birds wielding golf clubs. Yep, that's right. Whisky bottles shaped like birds, dressed in human clothes, swinging niblicks. It's a bit like finding a display case full of Smurfs in the Connaught. After you preprandial drink with the birds you are shown into one of a series of dining rooms of the utmost severity. You sit at a square black melamine-topped table and are given hot towels to wipe the hands and a little salad of cold flaked salmon and cucumber to tickle the palate. Graceful and beautiful waitresses, whose forte is not necessarily the Queen's English, glide across the room.

   The menu is a reasonably comprehensive account of

163

everything Japanese food fans adore. The sushi and sashimi are sparklingly fresh, well selected and, as always with Japanese food, beautifully presented. One of the best tasting steaks on earth arrives on a sizzling cast iron platter accompanied by bean sprouts and mushrooms. Those who loved being pampered will choose shabu shabu; a copper pot of broth simmers on your table and the waitress stands by, plunging in beef and vegetables and fishing them out as they cook. It is slow and glamorous eating. Some people will want to drink wine with Japanese food and this is a grave mistake: if you have a hard head drink sake, if not there is excellent beer 'canned in draught through micro-filtration'. Dessert is artfully dissected fruit. Your fellow diners – 90 per cent Japanese mugwumps in black suits – ain't a barrel of laughs and this establishment is not for knees-ups, but gosh the food is good.

Sweetings

39 Queen Victoria Street,
London EC4
Tel: 01-248 3062
Mon-Fri 11.30 to 3
NO CREDIT CARDS
££

> Good for: *Solitary lunches, comforting fish*
> Caveats: *Wear pinstripes*

As in so many other City institutions, the surface anarchy here disguises a smoothly running machine. This is one of the most lovable restaurants in London and probably one of the most successful as well. A bookingless establishment, you must arrive here very early – well before 12.30 or very late, 2ish, to get a seat – otherwise the wait is long. But it is not undiverting as you can watch visiting Japanese merchant bankers drink their first black velvets (served up in half pint or pint mugs) or observe 'barrow boys' from the financial markets scoffing quick sandwiches in the mosaic-floored bar. The impatient may forego the tiny dining room and perch on green leatherette stools in the bar: ideal for the solitary, too. The glossy buttercup-painted walls are hung with Spy prints. Tables are communal in the dining room. There are paper tablecloths, silver metal ice buckets and a traffic jam of condiments: Lea & Perrins, Tabasco, vinegar, plates of quartered lemons and sauceboats of tartar.

The menu is fish with a few concessions – ox tongue, ham on the bone – to the meat eater. Soups, such as leek and potato, are mundane and good: smoked salmon, soused herring, whitebait and potted shrimps are all exemplary. On lucky days you might have moules marinières served in neo-baroque silver-plated salvers and garnished with triangles of fried bread. Main courses are fish: fried, grilled or poached. Fried halibut is perfectly cooked and heroically proportioned, grilled plaice on the bone is sweet and *au point*, poached haddock is properly comforting. The salmon fishcakes are the best in town and the fish pie just the ticket for when you're feeling unloved or undernourished. The vegetables and salads play big parts. Puddings are arcane – Baidji figs? – and nostalgic. There is no coffee or tea, but you can linger over wine or port or Armagnac. A veteran team of mostly Spanish white-jacketed waiters cope and cosset with admirable efficiency. After lunch, the Temple of Mithras – neatly preserved in an office building forecourt – is a short and instructive stroll away.

La Tante Claire

68 Royal Hospital Road,
London SW3
Tel: 01-352 6045
Mon-Fri 12.30 to 2, 7 to 11
AMEX, DINERS
£££

> Good for: *Cheap lunches, special birthdays*
> Caveats: *Send besi suit to drycleaners*

This is one of the most justly celebrated restaurants in town; the chef, Pierre Kauffman, is a Roux brothers acolyte who, I feel, consistently outdoes his masters. The once long and narrow dining room has vanished, next door has been bought and the new premises are altogether lighter and nicer than what was before. A slimline hall leads to a small parquet floored bar where you can lounge on sofas and wait for your guests. The dining room somehow feels like New York's upper East Side, maybe because it contrives to be cosseting and characterless at the same time. Not, it must be said, that it's unpleasant: the pale woodwork, the chrome inlay, the Empire sidechairs even the modernistic light fixtures are all jolly nice, just a tiny bit soulless.

The short menu is enticing, exciting and boy-oh-boy-is-it-expensive. You will be given a splendidly inventive amuse-gueule – something like flawless charcuterie with a little lentil salad. First courses are nicely and unfussily presented on huge plates: you might have a splendid salad – designer leaves (like lamb's lettuce) liberally garnished with foie gras – or maybe a warm and forcibly flavoured hare mousseline with a wild mushroom sauce. Main courses neatly combine power and delicacy. Lightly cooked breast of wild duck sits on a potently flavourful

167

sauce accompanied by a dreamy circle of pommes dauphinoise. Fish is cooked with aplomb; slices of yellow tail are lightly sautéed and served on a bed of red pepper and ginger with a beautiful but unfussy garnish of criss-crossed carrots, broccoli and courgettes. The cheeseboard is magisterial and puddings, like a warm feuilleté of raspberries, sublime. The longish wine list includes a number of surpri-

singly affordable bottles. Service from nattily beblazered captains and white-jacketed waiters is dignified but helpful. You may eat surrounded by divorcees in Chanel and Concorde flyers, but this is one of the very few restaurants in London which provides serious, but notably unpretentious state-of-the-art cooking. The set lunch is a remarkably good deal.

The Tate Gallery Restaurant

Millbank,
London SW1
Tel: 01-834 6754
Mon-Sat 12 to 3
NO CREDIT CARDS
££

> Good for: *Cheap wine, upward mobility, pre-prandial culture*
> Caveats: *Careless cookery, lack of comfort*

Nowhere else could culture and fodder combine so happily. A visit to Hogarth's *The Dance* – surely the merriest painting in the history of English art – makes an ideal aperitif, then it's downstairs and into the cavernous restaurant stunningly bemuralled by Rex Whistler's 1927 fantasy *The Expedition in Pursuit of Rare Meats*. The clientele here is a neat mix of aging bon viveurs, gold-card American couples and earnest yuppies engaged in 'meetings'. The celebrated wine list attracts a lot of serious drinkers, but for a place where the Château Talbot '78 flows like water (and so it should at £16 a bottle) fellow lunchers looked a surprisingly healthy bunch. The wine list is indeed long, interesting and laden with bargains and curiosities, though in common with other establishments they seem to have problems getting half bottles of decent claret.

The menu, alas, combines the pedestrian with the unwanted: a large number of 'historic' recipes are dragged out of the culinary attic – Joan Cromwell's grand sallet could have been left to lie in decent obscurity. A first-course vegetarian gateau (*sic*) is available to the masochistic as a main course: stodgy, soggy and tasteless it could turn even the most hardened SDP member into a carnivore. Better to have the pedestrian tomato soup or the salmon mousse.

Indeed the menu is a torture to the adventurous. Hindle Wakes, 'an ancient poultry recipe from Lancashire dating back to medieval times', supports the theory that the Wars of the Roses may have been caused by indigestion. Cold sliced chicken with a prune stuffing tasting of nothing and accompanied by a salad that would disgrace a motorway service area ain't my idea of a medieval masterpiece. A simple daily special like roast beef is probably a better bet. Vegetables and potatoes are incompetent. Trifle is okay and there are farmhouse cheeses. Seating on black banquettes is comfortable enough, but this is one of those rare restaurants where every seat is the worst in the house. Service is, to be kind, extremely disorganised. Why the food here is quite so bad is a mystery. Still, it is pleasant enough to drink some nice wine without breaking the bank and admire the Rex Whistlers. For the more rushed or budget conscious there is a trendy circular snack bar designed by post-modernist Jeremy Dixon just across the hall.

Tiger Lee

251 Old Brompton Road,
London SW5
Tel: 01-370 2323
Mon-Sun 6 to 11
ACCESS, AMEX, DINERS, VISA
£££

Good for: *Continental visitors, Croesusian crustacea*
Caveats: *Rather dull*

This place seems to have a high reputation among restaurant guides and hall porters at expensive West End hotels. How else to explain the large numbers of cash-toting Americans or Cartier-clad Français who descend for dinner. The room is most peculiar: a cheerless celadon-painted rectangle reminiscent of a departure lounge in a Third World airport and the seats – big padded jobs which appear to have been salvaged from a 747 – owe more than a little to the Wright Brothers too. There is, thankfully, no life jacket demonstration. The tone – with foo lion chopstick rests and smartly tuxedoed waiters – is definitely high, as are the prices.

First courses are cooked with flair and served with finesse: roast prawns with green chillies are to the point and fillet of chicken in paper approaches Forbidden City standard. But, as in so many Oriental restaurants, the China Syndrome (meltdown of the menu) strikes with the main courses. Fish is a speciality here and the dover sole with spring onions is huge, perfectly cooked and nicely served. On the other hand a more mundane choice like beef with oyster sauce really is no better than at any other of hundreds of Chinese restaurants, even though the carrots are nicely carved like butterflies. Monks vegetables were decently cooked but utterly lacking in the sort of gastronomic zip that a restaurant of this standard ought to provide with every dish. Garnishes – one dish boasted a slice of lemon topped with a glacé cherry – can be slightly eccentric. I suppose that to get the best out of Tiger Lee one ought to stick to the fishy and go for broke with the lobsterish. In the wake of the growth of upmarket Chinese restaurants – of which this was one of the first – it does all feel and taste just a little bit irrelevant. Ladies are given a rose on the way out. House wine is drinkable and treated properly.

Topkapi

25 Marylebone High Street,
London W1
Tel: 01-486 1872
Mon-Sun 12 to 12
ACCESS, AMEX, DINERS, VISA
£

> Good for: *Casual dating, laid-back business lunching*
> Caveats: *Not for vampires – garlic overdose*

Turkish cooking is probably the most refined and complex of all the newly trendy Levantine cuisines. It will be a revelation to all of those who think that what the local kebab house produces – the same predictable litany of commercially produced taramasalata, chewy lamb kebabs and feta cheese salad – is the staple diet of all parts East. Although London's small Turkish community is fairly well served with local restaurants, there are sadly few Turkish places in the restaurant business mainstream and so far this splendid food has remained a minority interest. But the Topkapi, by virtue of excellent cooking, cheapish prices and a central location, has developed a popular following of which they are not a little proud. Indeed the long-winded accolade 'Capital Radio 194 Ad Lib Restaurant of the Year 1984 Overall Winner' is emblazoned on menu cover and front door. In spite of this mass acclaim it keeps an authentic flavour. You enter past a takeaway counter where busy chefs monitor the diurnal course of a large doner kebab and skewers of lamb and chicken repose in a refrigerator case. You might see swarthy men chain smoking and gulping raki (the astonishing strong white spirit of the Middle East). There is an enthusiastic if not entirely convincing mural of a Bosporean landscape, an array of glittering Turkish plates hanging on the wall and some fairly deft Arab calligraphy.

The menu is long on first courses and grills. There are excellent boreks (little triangles of puff pastry), delicious tiny meatballs and a refreshing cacik (a yoghurt and cucumber dip) which is described on the menu – as are the imam bayildi and stuffed eggplant – as being flavoured with a 'kiss of garlic'. They're being coy, the kiss of garlic here is more of a full-fledged bonking. The most successful main courses are variations on the grilled lamb or chicken theme served with rice pilaf, a little red cabbage and a fearsomely hot and utterly delicious red chilli sauce as an optional seasoning. The topkapi special ('secret recipe') grilled marinated chicken breast is a fine example of the grill master's art. The 'Special Dishes' (that is, not grilled) are less exciting: kuzu firin, 'lamb roasted in special oven', is downright boring. Helpings are huge, but the exceedingly robust may feel able to face the array of sticky sweet desserts. Service is efficient and solicitous. Villa doluca is a tasty enough Turkish white wine even if the bouquet is slightly reminiscent of a petrol station forecourt. A little card on each table advises that 'having enjoyed the finest Turkish cuisine why not plan your next holiday there with the best holiday specialist'.

Tui

19 Exhibition Road,
London SW7
Tel 01-584 8359
Mon-Sat 12 to 2.30, 6.30 to 11
Sun 12.30 to 2.30, 7 to 10.30
ACCESS, AMEX, DINERS, VISA
££

> Good for: *Sunday nights after country weekends*
> Caveats: *Some odd tables*

Hot, weird and interesting, Thai food is the Oriental of the
future, but its culinary fashionability is rarely reflected by
London's Thai restaurants, which tend to be a dowdy even
though worthy bunch. This place stands out both for the
excellence of its cooking and for the chic of its presentation, no wonder it's been a roaring success since day one.
Location helps too: the heart of South Kensington boasts
few decent restaurants. What could make a nicer morning
than an amble through the V&A followed by a blast of Thai
chilli and a few Singha beers? This tiny two-decker establishment feels like an ocean liner decorated by Busby Ber-
keley. There are plenty of art deco touches, like the smart
black stained woodwork, the round windows in the doors
and the slick Italian chrome ware. The quarry tile floor is
muted grey, the chairs fake Mallet Stevens and the ceiling
fans painted matt black – a far cry from the decorative
excesses or dullness of most Oriental restaurants. Alas,
some of the tables – near the door or in the middle of the
room – are expedient rather than comfortable.

The menu is a lengthy and stimulating catalogue of ferociously unpronounceable dishes with concise English
explanations. First courses are presented on smart rectang-

ular celadon plates, neatly adorned with intricately carved carrots. (The Thais are outstanding food carvers.) Some of the food is simple street vendor style like succulent grilled marinated chicken served with a sweet chilli sauce. There are excellent prawns in breadcrumbs lightly and precisely fried. Curiously the sateh, though perfectly decent, is mildly disappointing. There is a first-rate selection of soups served from rather battered aluminium pots with a built-in heater and a chimney running up the middle. My favourite is tam yum gai, a vigorously spiced chicken and straw mushroom soup flecked with red chilli, ideal for cold days or sluggish minds. Mee grob, crisp noodles with tamarind sauce, is well done but tastes slightly like something you might eat in a Thai cinema. Seasonal vegetables (pud puk) are high quality, crisply cooked and subtly sauced. At lunch they do a fastish food noodle menu featuring one-dish lunches like angels hair noodles with Thai-style beef. Ice cream is the most soothing pudding. You can drink wine but the excellent Thai beer is better. Service by well-dressed waiters and waitresses is graceful and friendly.

TODAY'S MENU
La Belle SARDINE
STRIP-TEASE

APICELLA 87

The Veeraswamy

99-101 Regent Street,
London W1
Tel: 01-734 1401
Mon-Sat 12 to 2.30, 6 to 11.30
Sun 12 to 2.30, 7 to 10.30
ACCESS, AMEX, DINERS, VISA
££

> Good for: *Lively flavours, vegetables*
> Caveats: *Not for the faint hearted*

This is the oldest Indian restaurant in town. 'Founded in 1927,' the menu relates, 'by Edward Palmer, grandson of Lieutenant General William Palmer and the daughter of the Nizam of Hyderabad' – not a bad pedigree. In recent years it became a sad caricature of Indian cooking. Thankfully new management stepped in to take advantage of the splendid site and unimpeachable history. Alas, in the process the wonderfully kitschy Kashmiri decor was lost. Not that the new scheme looks bad at all with salmon pinks and greys, beautiful tiles and comfortable *Directoire* fauteuils. You pass through the by-now-*de-rigueur*-in-any-upmarket-Indian restaurant cocktail bar into the dining room nicely perched above Regent Street – window tables get excellent views.

The long and appetising menu is printed on grey marbled paper. First courses, they call them (cringe) 'good beginnings', shy away from the run-of-the-mill. Alu Tikki, best described as an Indian bubble and squeak with mashed potatoes, lentils and green chilli, is served in a tidy heap topped with date, tamarind and mint chutneys. Fresh and snappy it's one of the best Indian first courses in London. The shrimp masala with coconut doesn't beat

around the bush either. Even the most conventional-sounding main courses are a cut above most of the better Indian restaurants in London. Rogan josh, lamb stew with yoghurt, is flavourful and made with top-class ingredients. Chicken tikka comes in a jaunty mint coat. There are more arcane offerings, too, like brain masala – 'worth trying' quoth the menu. Vegetarians are well served by two mag-

APICELLA '86

nificent thalis (a selection of vegetables served in little metal bowls), the punjabi and gujerati. The punjabi includes an arresting dish of colocasia – a sort of yam – sautéed with mango and pomegranate. Throughout, flavours are fresh, spices are forthright. There is a range of Indian puddings and sorbets. Service is friendly and less otherworldly than some Indian restaurants. Coffee is horrible. This must strongly challenge the Bombay Brasserie as the best Indian restaurant in town if the management and kitchen can sustain the early days enthusiasm. Fellow diners include some Sloane Ranger Indians.

Walton's

121 Walton Street,
London SW3
Tel: 01-584 0204
Mon-Sat 12.30 to 2.30, 7.30 to 11.30
Sun 12.30 to 2, 7.30 to 10
ACCESS, AMEX, DINERS, VISA
£££

Good for: *Visiting continentals, seduction dinners* Caveats: *Unrelaxing*

Formal, posh and ever so slightly stilted, Walton's is the doyen of Walton Street restaurants, looking a bit disdainfully at its neighbours. After all, it was here before Walton Street became part of the ultra-fashionable perhaps slightly factitious neighbourhood now dubbed Brompton Cross. The look of the place is certainly a million miles away from the cod bonhomie of the Brasserie or the sleek minimalism of Joe's Café (*q.v.* L'Express). This is the grown-up streaked blonde mistress look applied to restaurants. An imposing acreage of mirrors, quilted yellow under-tablecloths, chrome-plated chairs with cane seats, a sail loft full of grey drapery and little globular lamps all comprise a perfect essay in mid-seventies tart's boudoir design. The vulvic flower prints are an extra. Cookery here strives towards the naughty and slightly perverse as well.

The number of menus – 'Simply Walton's', 'Lunch', 'Dinner', 'Walton's Supper' – could perplex even the most sedulous of bureaucrats. The menu language – 'First Dishes', 'Second Dishes', 'Principal Dishes' – approaches the Firbankian. In spite of all these warning signs the cooking is good if sometimes rather baffling. Salad of grapefruit, avocado and artichokes is skilfully presented, but really rather unnecessary. A terrine of dover sole with a saffron colour mousse sadly sounds and looks better than it tastes. Soups are good. Main courses – oops sorry, 'principal dishes' – might confound the plain man. Pan-fried calves' liver comes with (yucch) citrus fruits; an innocent breast of chicken is – bad idea *par excellence* – stuffed with salmon. The equally silly-sounding chicken with oysters is rather good though it has a tendency towards over-refined blandness. Fish is treated well. Steamed halibut with an aromatic sauce is good quality fish respectfully cooked. Vegetables are excellent. In common with other 'English' restaurants puddings are glorious, but best shared. Service is deferential, irritatingly distant and therefore just a tiny bit annoying. The wine list makes wonderful reading; less good drinking for the non-plutocratic. The £11.00 set lunch is a very good deal indeed. I can't help thinking that this sort of cooking, with its emphasis on outlandish liaisons and exquisite presentation, is more than slightly irrelevant, but there is certainly no shortage of well-heeled – either smartly coiffed or beblazered – patrons here.

The White Tower

1 Percy Street,
London W1
Tel: 01-636 8141
Mon-Fri 12.30 to 2.30, 6.30 to 10.30
ACCESS, AMEX, DINERS, VISA
££

Good for: *Grills, dignity*
Caveats: *Menu writer's mouth*

The White Tower is comfortably reminiscent (along with its
near neighbour L'Etoile) of the days when North Soho (or is
it South Fitzrovia?) was raffish and 'foreign'. This of course
was long before moussaka and chips were staples of the
British diet or taramasalata was stocked in every delicatessen. Indeed, gastronomic innocence is most strongly
evoked by the menu's description of taramasalata as 'pâté'.

The chatty and anecdotal menu makes good reading for
the lone diner or student of pidgin English sales patter: 'The
pilaf is a dish of infinite variety and charm. There are as
many ways of making a pilaf as there are of playing Hamlet
. . . or Don Quixote'. 'Once upon a time there lived in Asia
Minor a famous Imam. He was inordinately fond of food.
His particular weakness was the aubergine cooked in no
matter which of its various delectable forms . . .' 'Created
for those of our friends who like to try outlandish dishes but
are somewhat conservative in their taste . . .' Lovers of the
outlandish might want to try saganaki à la perea; not the
innocent plate of fried cheese we might think, but an astonishing concoction of fried scampi, artichoke hearts and
mushrooms, rather like an hors d'oeuvre trolley struck by
napalm. Better stick to the fresh simplicity of fish salad
(turbot dressed with oil, lemon and chopped onion) or egg

lemon soup ('guaranteed to warm the cockles of your heart'). Main courses can be muddled. Assiette kalomyra (poached chicken, courgette, rice and a sauce made with – you guessed it – 'new-laid eggs') is bland and sloppy like invalid food. Chicken paxinou (chicken fried with bananas and aubergines) must be the product of an inexplicable urge to 'create'. The charcoal-grilled food (veal, lamb, calves' liver, steak, chicken) is splendid and uncheap. The fish kebab is pretty hot stuff too.

This must be one of the first of the 'upmarket' ethnic restaurants which London is now so well supplied with. Like all grand establishments of forty years ago there is a vast and hierarchical staff and the seating is a paragon of discretion: you sit side by side and the tables are divided by glass panels – handy for protection against sneezes, cigar smoke and unwanted confidences. The dark green upstairs dining room with its glowering portrait of Lord Byron is ideal for a cosseting and rather anachronistic escape from the culinary and other anxieties of the eighties. Fellow customers will be aging, rich and rather quiet. Service is charming.

The Wine Gallery

49 Hollywood Road,
London SW10
Tel: 01-352 7572
Mon-Sat 12 to 3, 7 to 12
Sun 12 to 2, 7 to 11
ACCESS, VISA
£

Good for: *Jolly fodder, late nights, funky Sunday lunch*
Caveats: *Noisy, crowded, not for Labour party members*

Through a haze of Silk Cuts, din of fwah-fwah voices and flurry of furiously backcombed hair, a first-rate neighbourhood restaurant can be discerned. Hollywood Road is the mecca for the jeunesse hooray of London SW10 and John Brinkley's estimable establishment is their prime watering hole. The setting is basic: lino floors, scrubbed wooden tables and walls densely hung with a variety of pictures for sale – which are sometimes good, often rather mediocre. The young and noisy crowd around the bar; the slightly more grown-up favour the garden side, and downstairs seems to attract either the amorous or else small gaggles seeking post-drinks party or maybe pre-dance ballast.

The menu is a fairly inspired blend of the snackish and the more complicated; so you can dawdle over a bacon, lettuce and tomato sandwich or go the whole hog. The food is surprisingly good and better yet it is remarkably consistent. A quite smart first course like timbale of scallops with lobster sauce is tasty and well executed; there appears to be an inexhaustible supply of good globe artichokes and the soups (with the exception of highly disappointing gazpacho) taste like the proper home-made thing. Avocado with sour cream and Danish caviar is sloppy and satisfying rather than finely tuned – quite a young married's dinner party dish. Main courses tend towards competent, honest interpretations of nursery food: sausages, beans and mash, fishcakes, kedgeree. But they also do a line in more progressive cooking with good monkfish and chips, gravadlax and smoked chicken and melon salad. Puddings like lime mousse and crème brûlée are gooey and good. The wine list is concise and well priced: house wine is £4.80 and for slightly more you can get something interesting like Bulgarian chardonnay or an Australian cabernet shiraz. Service is of the casual but somehow efficient school. Prices are astonishingly low, the food and drink are good if not world beating and most people appear to be enjoying themselves. Small wonder that there are three Wine Galleries. Every neighbourhood should have one.

Zen

Chelsea Cloisters,
Sloane Avenue,
London SW3
Tel: 01-589 1781
Mon-Fri 12 to 3, 6 to 11.15
Sat 12 to 11.15
Sun 12 to 11
ACCESS, AMEX, DINERS, VISA
££

> Good for: *Second marriage proposals, thoughtful vegetarians*
> Caveats: *Wear biggest costume jewellry*

Lawrence Leung, owner of this place and quite a few others, is in the Chinese film business, which may explain the flamboyance of the decor. Zen doesn't have ideas above its station but clearly has major aspirations, as the sign proclaiming 'Chinese Cuisine' hints. Through the front door and you're greeted by a miniature waterfall cascading over a boulder set into the wall: the next-door table is not for the weak of bladder. This is a small bar with a floppy 'sectional' sofa. The dining room is pure oriental glitz with paintings of the signs of the Chinese Zodiac and a vast acreage of mirrored ceiling and pillar. Seating is at large round tables with comfortable chairs and rust-coloured nappery.

The chopstick-cum-spoon-rests are astonishingly elaborate, as is the menu. The most conservative second-hand car salesman could construct a comforting lunch or dinner here but the more adventurous will be better rewarded. Stuffed squid with Szechuan peppercorns and salt is perhaps less exciting than it sounds, but nonetheless good lightly fried squid. The enticing coriander croquettes are more like patrician cocktail snacks. Scallops with black bean sauce served on the half shell are deftly cooked and spectacular looking. You can have the standard crispy duck with pancakes; tea-smoked duck is more unusual and flavourful even if the mysteries of Chinese butchery remain unsolved afterwards. Crab for the affluent and lobster for the rich are both neatly cooked. Steamed fish, either dover sole or sea bass, is absolutely *au point*. Monks vegetables, a farrago of mangetout, fungi and bean curd, are served on a highly decorated stand concealing a warming candle. Hard-core vegetarians can take advantage of more arcane bean curd dishes. Fresh fruit – maybe sliced melon on a bed of ice cubes – makes the best pudding. The wine list is probably the most distinguished of any Chinese restaurant in London. Contrary to the Chinese restaurant norm, service is engaging though not always comprehensible. Maitre d's wear dinner jackets, most customers fall slightly short of that sartorial standard, but it is unusual to see a tieless man.

ZenW3, the sister establishment in Hampstead, has equally high culinary intentions and slightly more modern cooking with an emphasis on grilling and steaming. Clientele and decor are flashier (N.B. the gold chains on the men and the water flowing down the staircase handrail).

Ziani

45-47 Radnor Walk,
London SW3
Tel: 01-352 2698
Mon-Sun 12.30 to 2.45, 7 to 11.30
ACCESS, AMEX, DINERS, VISA
££

> Good for: *Gregarious lunches/dinners, grilled fish*
> Caveats: *Noisy/smokey neighbours*

Judicious menu reading can provide the best part of a liberal education: at Ziani it's Venetian history 101. 'The Venetian republic was a glittering phenomenon. Fabulously wealthy, the Ziani were popularly believed to have derived their wealth from a golden cow discovered in an ancestor's cellar.' Golden cow or not, Sebastiano Ziani – namesake of this establishment – was rich and a good egg to boot. Generations of tourists are unconsciously grateful for this late twelfth-century doge who gave the Piazza San Marco its modern form.

With so much history on the menu it is unsurprising that Ziani is a Venetian restaurant. What is surprising, though, is that Venetian restaurants (*q.v.* Santini) should open in London: the Serene Republic is, alas, not noted for its food. Even so, Ziani is a welcome social (not just local hoorays, but even royals have munched here) and gastronomic adornment to the fairly dismal wasteland of London Italian restaurants. It is jolly hard to get into – the entrance is so cunningly tucked around the corner that without due care you could end up in the neighbour's sitting room. In the modern Italian restaurant style there are white walls and bentwood chairs and baskets of hanging ivy where once Chianti bottles would have dangled. There is of course an acreage of venetian blinds. Tables are so close together that even the incurious will pick up details of their fellow diners' divorce proceedings, stock options and plans for the weekend. The pasta can be very good indeed. Rosette, disc-shaped pasta stuffed with spinach and ricotta, were perfectly cooked and gently sauced with a sparkingly fresh tomato sauce. Even the most banal items like mixed anti-pasto – a huge conglomeration of artichokes, seafood salad, radicchio, prosciutto and tonno e fagioli – are carefully prepared and far from the tired war horses that haunt so many Italian menus. Fish figures heavily here and the mixed grill, which may have sole, salmon, monkfish and squid, is an excellent and dauntingly huge sampler. Fritto misto is fresh and crisp as well. The more austere could have bass cooked in foil. Salads and vegetables are average. A trolley laden with the usual array of puddings lurks for the ravenous. Service by yellow-shirted waiters has brio but stops short of the opera buffa.

Index

GOOD FOR . . .